CRIME OF PASSION:

murder and
the murderer

David Lester
and Gene Lester

Crime of passion:

murder and the murderer

 Nelson-Hall Chicago

Lester, David, 1942-
    Crime of passion: murder and the murderer

    Bibliography: p.
    Includes index.
    1. Murder. 2. Homicide 3. Suicide. I. Lester,
Gene, 1941- joint author. II. Title.
HV6515.L4   364.1'523   74-20788

ISBN: 0-88229-139-4

Contents

200
physical
psychological

Preface

Aggression, anger, and hostility are expressed by human beings in ways which range from sarcasm to saturation bombing. Some hostile acts are committed by a single individual, while others are a consequence of group solidarity. Theories about the sources of aggression try to find similar motives for all these varied actions. In many ways, we have come to feel that concepts about aggression are best tested by consideration of the simplest, most clear-cut aggressive act—murder of one person by one other person. The idea for this book on murder, the Crime of Passion, arose from an interest in the general problem of aggression.

The act of murder is clearly defined by the death of one of the participants; it generally occurs within a restricted and measurable period of time; the act itself, or at least its consequences, is observable by people other than the participants; and it is rarely arguable that the principal motivation for the act is anything other than aggression.

A great deal is known about murder though little is clearly understood. Its importance as a matter of special concern has caused modern bureaucracy to compile myriad data on such points as the age, sex, and occupation of murderers and their victims. Such information, dry as it may seem on the surface, is essential for the understanding of the complex actions of human beings. When each individual case of murder is colored by the special characteristics of that killer and his victim, we need many cases to allow us to average out individual differences and see the basic factors which all murders have in common. Those cases and information about them are readily available in acts of murder, as is not always true for other acts of aggression. (Even in war, as we have learned from Vietnam, body counts are often rather inaccurate. But woe betide the city police department which is found to have distorted its announcements of the murder rate in the way that armies sometimes do.)

Some special kinds of murder caught our attention particularly. Matricide, the killing of one's own mother, is an act which has held a mythical fascination throughout mankind's history. It is an excellent paradigm of the interpersonal stresses which so often cause murderers to choose friends or relatives as their victims. Infanticide, the killing of one's child, held a particular interest because it is so contrary to the general tendency among mammals to care for and protect the helpless young of their species and also because it is so often a reflection of the greater social problem of population control. Genocide, the killing off of an entire racial or cultural group, demands attention in the light of the history of the present century.

In addition to discussing these special forms of murder, we have presented information on the epidemiology of murder—the simple but crucial data which describe who kills whom, when, where, how, and why. As the reader will see, the reality of the statistics about murder presents a rather different picture from the usual stereotype of the killer.

A discussion of the legal aspects of murder forms another important chapter. Not all killings are murder. The law decides which ones shall be labeled as murders (a fact which helps determine the statistics about murder). In our culture, the killing of a fleeing suspect by a policeman is not legally murder; in some other cultures, killing of one's newborn infant for purposes of population control is not considered murder. Killing by a public executioner is a responsibility, not a crime. Killing as a result of accident or negligence does not fall within the legal definition of murder either. Complex questions of volition, rationality, and sanity all enter into the process of defining murder.

The statistics of murder without some case studies would give the reader an incomplete picture of the complex and individual nature of the motivation to kill another person. Therefore we have included a number of case histories—some given in brief as illustrations of concepts, some with entire chapters and complete discussions devoted to them. We have tried to use the case histories to illustrate the idea of deep interpersonal stresses behind every case of murder.

That there are two kinds of murderers is a central

concept of this book. We have compared killings which result from *undercontrolled* aggression, in individuals whose tendency to get into brawls eventually culminates in a murder, and *overcontrolled* aggression, in persons whose inability to express anger appropriately leads to mounting stress and a complete loss of control sometimes resulting in a brutal murder. The differences between the undercontrolled and the overcontrolled murderer have a number of implications for social attitudes and for legal treatment of the killer.

This book is intended primarily for the student and for the layman. With this audience in mind, we have tried always to offer definitions and explanations of unusual words and concepts. However, we think our work will also be useful for the professional, because we have brought together a great deal of information which until now was available only in original papers or in edited volumes. There is, in fact, no other modern book which attempts to organize and discuss the available research as we have done. We have also added commentary and discussion on many of the cases drawn from the existing literature.

part 1

Introduction to murder

Chapter 1

Murder : myth and reality

Murder is an action difficult for nonmurderers to understand. Although most people have felt the prickings of rage and resentment that could prompt them to desire another's death, they recoil at the thought of killing and feel themselves physically incapable of murder. Even those who imagine the victim's neck between their hands, the cocked gun aimed at the pleading enemy, or the strychnine dissolving in the soup still shrink away from actual murderous plans and vaguely desire to avoid even the possibility of killing. Yet murders are committed in surprising numbers—in this decade about 10,000 every year in the United States. How do the murderers overcome that feeling of revulsion? Or do they never have the feeling at all? Are they from an early age different in personality from nonmurders? The answers to these questions, which we will deal with in this book, are necessary for some understanding of murder.

The apparent incomprehensibility of murder may in part be explained by the common misconceptions about the act. The average person's concept of murder is drawn in equal parts from murder mysteries and from lurid newspaper accounts of dramatic killings. These sources give rise to a number of mistaken beliefs.

In the stereotyped scenario, the killer is motivated by the desire for gain. He may want to rob his victim, or he may expect to inherit the victim's possessions or to be the beneficiary of an insurance policy. The murderer is the kind of person who would rather kill to gain a fortune than work for and save money the way other people do. He is clever and patient, though, and he bides his time while he plots and plans his act over a period of months or years. When the murder is finally carried out, it is performed with steady nerves—"in cold blood." Strangely, though the murderer has planned his killing for so long, his act comes as a complete surprise to other people. Nothing about the murderer's behavior gives him away or would allow anyone to predict the killing. One of the reasons for this unpredictability is the lack of close contact between murderer and victim; they are strangers or distant acquaintances. Another reason is that the murderer is insane, and his behavior cannot be predicted like that of normal people. His twisted mind must be the result of some inherited flaw, for he comes from a respectable family which brought him up carefully and lovingly without ever guessing what disgrace he would some day bring upon them.

The reality of murder gives us a rather different picture.

Real murderers are not usually motivated by any long-range plans or conscious desires. Most commonly, they kill during some trivial quarrel, or their acts are triggered by some apparently unimportant incident, while deep and unconscious emotional needs are their basic motivation. Most murders occur on sudden impulse and in the heat of passion, in situations where the killer's emotions overcome his ability to reason. Since the motivation for murder is a matter of chronic needs and consistent aspects of the murderer's personality, it is possible to predict which people are most likely to kill. Prediction is also made feasible by the fact that most murders are preceded by periods of stress and crisis. The murderer's responses to stress can be observed, and he acts differently from his usual self for a few days before the murder. The stresses involved are usually interpersonal, a fact which helps explain why most killers are friends or relatives of their victims.

Some murderers, of course, are severely disturbed emotionally, but most are only mildly disturbed in their thoughts and feelings. The kinds of disturbances they show are usually related to their ability to obtain love from other people and to defend themselves against others' hostility. In addition, the killers are not usually consciously aware of their emotional needs, which are too frightening in their raw power to be experienced directly. These characteristics occur as a result of unusual childhood experiences of emotional rejection, physical cruelty, and accidental physical hurt.

Murder as a problem

If one considers the possibility of the victim's motivational contribution to murder, it may be that not all such killings are undesirable from the victim's point of view. However, most deaths by murder surely would be deplored by the victim (if he were in a position to do so), by the victim's relatives, and by society in general. This is especially true when the murderer is a stranger, when the murderer is emotionally disturbed and/or sadistic, and when the choice of victim is apparently random.

Assassination is a special type of murder which is distressing and, in addition, which may actually be dangerous to a country's political stability. These latter forms of murder are the ones which people are most likely to consider a problem. Murder between spouses or relatives is generally of great concern only to the family and a few friends. Unfortunately, random murders and assassinations are the least susceptible to control of all killings—and these murders are the ones which almost everyone would consider it desirable to prevent.

The sources of murder

The study of human aggression has provided many concepts and theories which are relevant to murder, though it has not given concrete answers to most commonly asked questions. The conceptual frameworks developed in the study of aggression are important, however, since they have stimulated and oriented research on murder. There are three major psychological theories within which murder has been investigated.

1. The psychoanalytic stance views violence as a natural human motivation whose expression is determined by the course of an individual's personality development. In addition, psychoanalysts feel that the motivation for a murder may have little to do with the objective relationship between murderer and victim, but

instead may be based upon a symbolic representation of the relationship between the murderer and a parent or other important person.

2. The frustration-aggression hypothesis suggests that the motivation for any violent aggressive action is produced by the blocking of an individual's access to his desired goals. Aggression may be turned against the real source of the frustration or against some easy substitute victim, as is the case when economic frustrations lead to an increase in activities like lynching.

3. The ethological position sees aggression as an inevitable characteristic of man's behavior. Aggressiveness is seen as a constantly building force which must be discharged in some way. Murder can occur when certain basic, biologically determined characteristics come into play—for example, as some have suggested, when personal territory is violated.

Sociological and anthropological thinking has made many contributions to the study of murder. For our purposes, however, the most important contribution may be the idea that the occurrence of murder depends upon cultural traditions. Murder in one society may be tolerated or even approved under certain conditions, whereas other cultures or subcultures may have quite different opinions, and, therefore, quite different patterns of murder. A lower-class American youth who kills in a gang fight may not be rebelling and/or acting out conflicts with his parents; he may instead be behaving as a proper citizen of his gang society.

Murderers and victims

Much research on murder has concentrated on the kind of person who kills and the circumstances under which the killing occurs. In recent years, however, there has been growing interest in the characteristics of the murder victim and in the relationship between murderer and victim. One concept growing out of this interest is described as victim-precipitated homicide. Some victims, it appears, are as strongly motivated to be killed as their murderers are to kill. The role of the victim is also apparent in infanticide, in which the demands and needs of the child may create stress too great for an immature parent to cope with. These ideas appear especially important when one remembers that most murders involve people who know each other. Rather than being an isolated event, the killing is most likely to be an integral part of the pattern of their relationship.

Understanding murder through research

Misconceptions about murder exist because relatively little good, systematic research has been done. Although, as we pointed out in the preface, it is possible to obtain a great number of raw data about murder, a number of considerations have hampered research. The reality of the study of murder includes the problems of research.

Although 10,000 murders a year may well be thought of as 10,000 too many, murder is a relatively infrequent act with respect to the population as a whole. Twice as many suicides as murders have occurred each year in the recent past, and deaths from other causes (like accidents) are much more common. A rare behavior is more difficult to study than a frequent one simply because appropriate cases are difficult to obtain.

The statistics of murder are dependent on legal considerations, since not every killing of a human being is counted as murder. Even when killings in war, accidental killings, and justifiable homicide by law officers are excluded, one finds that murder is differently defined in different states and countries and in different times. The extent to which juries decide that given killings match the current local definition of murder is even more variable than the laws themselves.

Many murderers are chronically angry and over-concerned about their rights and their treatment by others. Such people are not likely to cooperate with researchers.

It is inaccurate to assume that all prisoners kill for the same reasons. The act of murder can probably be motivated in a number of different ways. Such differences further reduce the number of murderers appropriate and available for investigation in any one study.

Sources of information about murder

Where does a researcher go to find the basic raw data about murder? Such information is available in the well-filled archives of governmental agencies, hospitals, clinics, schools, and psychotherapists. Records about causes of death, about court cases, and about social problems are compiled and kept by the bureaucracies of all the developed nations. An important source of information in this country is the Uniform Crime Reports of the Federal Bureau of Investigation, which provides national, state, and local statistics on crimes reported to the police. Court documents and transcripts of trials are a source of information about motivation for murder and such questions as the sanity of killers. Juvenile court records, too, show the past history of violent or disturbed behavior in adults who murder. Similarly, the records of hospitals and of examining psychiatrists can be correlated with murder. There is a great deal of information in existence; the problem, of course, is searching it out and finding the pattern in its complexity.

FIGURE 1

HOMICIDE RATES FOR
THE DEATH-REGISTRATION AREA, 1900-64.*

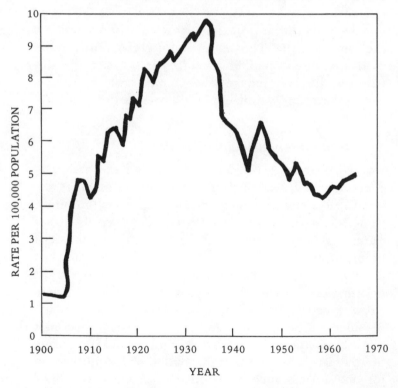

*From Langberg (1967, p. 2)

Chapter 2

My brother's killer:
the statistics

Murder, like other human behaviors, does not often occur at random. Definite patterns of characteristics tend to apply to the victims, the killers, the methods, and the places of death. In the present chapter, we are going to describe some of the statistical evidence about the act of murder.

The available evidence is not complete, particularly with reference to certain aspects. Less is known about the characteristics of the murderers than about the victims because a number of murderers do not get arrested or, if arrested, are not found guilty or sentenced. Even for the murder victims, the information is not complete, for some undetected murders are classified as accidental or natural deaths or as suicides. Nonetheless, the great majority of murders are probably classified correctly. This allows the compiling of correct information about the victim, the method of murder, and the time and place of death. We will begin by dealing with the known characteristics of murder victims.

THE VICTIMS

Frequency of deaths

A wide variation in the U. S. homicide rate during this century has been reported by Langberg (1967). The rate was quite low in 1900 (about 1 per 100,000 per year), but it rose to a peak of about 10 per 100,000 per year in the 1930s. Since then, the rate has fallen to about 5 per 100,000 per year. The variation of the rates over time is shown in figure 1.

A number of complicating factors may be partially responsible for the variation in the murder rate. For one thing, not all of the states reported murder statistics to the federal authorities in 1900. Only the statistics after 1933 refer to the whole of the continental United States. Some of the variation prior to 1933 may be due to the first reports of states which had not previously been included. Of course, many of the states which began reporting at that time would have been southern states and western states which had just been admitted to the Union. Both of these factors would have contributed to a high homicide rate, especially in the earlier part of the century. Another contributing factor was probably Prohibition. The peak of the homicide rate coincided with the period of Prohibition, when organized crime and gangland murders were also at a peak.

General characteristics of the victims

Considerably more men than women die from homicide. The age-adjusted rates (rates corrected for the fact that the groups being compared differ in their distribution of ages) for 1959-61 were 7.8 per 100,000 per year for males and 2.6 per 100,000 per year for females.

People in certain age groups are much more likely to be murdered than those in other groups. The rates for different age groups in 1959-61 are shown in table 1.

TABLE 1

Yearly deaths by murder at different ages

Age Group	Rate per 100,000
0-1	4.6
1-4	0.9
5-14	0.6
15-24	8.9
25-34	14.3
35-44	12.2
45-54	9.6
55-64	6.6
65-74	4.7
75-84	3.9
85 +	3.8

Nonwhites are much more likely to be murdered than whites. The rates per 100,000 for 1959-61 (again age-adjusted) were 2.7 for whites and 25.2 for nonwhites.

The danger of metropolitan life is not substantiated by murder statistics. The chances of death from murder are almost exactly the same in metropolitan and nonmetropolitan areas (5.2 and 5.1 respectively). Nor do immigrant groups seem to have more murders than the native-born (both rates are 2.6).

As in the case for many other deviant behaviors, murder victims were more commonly found among those who were single, widowed, or divorced than among the married. The age-adjusted rates for single people were 10.7; for the widowed 19.9; for the divorced 21.5; and for the married only 5.4. (Comparing the murder rate among people with various marital statuses permits one to see the effects of age-adjustment, since, of course, single people are more likely to be younger and widows to be older. Without adjusting for these age differences, the rates are quite different: 7.5, 5.1, 21.8, and 5.3 respectively.)

The region in which a person lives makes a difference in the likelihood that he will be murdered. The age-adjusted rates for 1959-61 for different regions of the United States are shown in table 2.

TABLE 2

Regional murder rates per year

Region	Rate per 100,000
New England	1.5
Middle Atlantic	3.2
East North Central	3.9
West North Central	2.9
South Atlantic	9.2
East South Central	9.6
West South Central	8.3
Mountain	4.9
Pacific	4.1

Special victim groups

The reader may have noted, in looking at the age distribution of murder victims, that children under the age of one year are murdered much more often than older children. The murder of young children seems to be a special phenomenon which differs considerably from the murder of adults, as far as sex and race distributions are concerned. Rather than the considerable preponderance of males found in adult samples of murder victims, one finds among infants that an approximately equal number of boys and girls are killed. Like nonwhite adults, nonwhite children are murdered more frequently than whites, but the difference for children is not as great as that for adults. Whereas the murder rate for whites of all ages is 2.7 as compared to 22.9 for nonwhites, the rate for white children under the age of one year is 4.3 as compared to the rate for nonwhite children of 11.1.

The homicide rate for infants has been rising steadily since 1958 and is now about 60 percent higher than the 1958 level. It will be interesting to see whether the increase in the legal availability of abortion will decrease the rate of infant murder.

Another group in which the murder rate is relatively high is that of American Indians (Ogden, Spector, and Hill, 1970). Death from murder is much more common among Indians than in the general population of the United States. Age-adjusted rates for 1964 showed a murder rate of 5.8 in the general population and of 23.6 in the Indian population. The age and sex distribution of deaths by murder is similar for Indian groups and for the general population. The American Indian murder rate has also shown a rise between 1960 and 1967, paralleling a similar rise in the general population.

The average murder victim

Omitting the cases of small infants, one can picture the person who is most likely to be murdered. He is male, nonwhite, and not living with a spouse. He is most likely to be in the age range 25-34 years and to live in the southern part of the country. He is equally likely to live in a city or in the country. The person who is least likely to be murdered as an adult is a married woman over the age of 75 living in New England.

THE MURDERER

The distribution of sexes and races among murderers is, curiously enough, rather similar to that found among murder victims. According to Wolfgang (1958), who studied 588 homicides in Philadelphia in the years 1948-52, the rates of murder by each race and sex were the following:

Negro males	41.7
Negro females	9.3
Caucasian males	3.4
Caucasian females	0.4

However, the murderers tended to be younger than the victims. The median age of the murderers was 31.9 years and that of the victims 35.1 years. The highest frequency of committing murder occurred in the group aged 20-24, while the largest proportion of murder victims was found in the age group 25-34.

About two-thirds of the murderers had previous police records (as did about half the victims). The majority of the previous arrests were for offenses against people rather than property, which suggests that some of the murderers were habitually violent and quarrelsome.

The IQs of murderers

Berg and Fox (1947), who studied 200 male murderers, found an average score of 83 on the Army Alpha Test, which is comparable to the general population score of 89. Ranked with other kinds of criminals, the murderers had a lower IQ and a lower grade placement. There was no difference in IQ between the violent and nonviolent homicides, or between those who were habitually aggressive and those with no prior record of assault. Nor were there differences between murderers of male and female victims, or between drunk and sober murderers.

It has been proposed that criminals should have higher performance IQs (scores on mathematics and problem solving) than verbal IQs. The rationale for this idea was that performance requires less impulse inhibition than do verbal skills, and criminals are poor at inhibiting impulses. In a group of murderers, performance IQs were not consistently higher than verbal IQs (Kahn, 1968). However, Kahn did find that murderers with different psychiatric diagnoses had different IQs. Those diagnosed as sociopaths or as having character disorders had significantly lower verbal IQs than the other murderers in the sample.

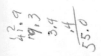

Murder and constitutional factors

We have noted in chapter 13 that murderers are often found to have abnormal brain electrical activity. Sayed, Lewis, and Brittain (1969) found abnormal electroencephalograms (EEGs) in 66 percent of their sample of murderers. They found that particular characteristics of brain activity were correlated with the degree of violence used in the murder, with the number of victims (one or more), and with the victim's kinship to the murderer. If these associations proved valid, they would be of great interest and difficult to explain.

Stafford-Clark and Taylor (1949) felt that abnormal EEGs were found most often in murderers who had no motive, who were insane, and for whom killing was associated with sexual satisfaction; and least often in the perpetrators of murders which were incidental or motivated. Bonkalo (1967), too, found that motiveless but sane murderers had more abnormal EEGs than motivated murderers. There was a high incidence of epileptics among the motiveless murderers, but since the violent acts rarely occurred during seizures or post-ictal confusion states, there was no implication that the murders were involuntary or unconscious.

In a poorly controlled study, Chrzanowski and Szymusik (1970) found that eleven of sixteen murderers they studied showed atrophy of subcortical parts of the brain.

The genetic abnormalities found in the sex chromosomes of murderers are discussed in detail in chapter 13. The XYY syndrome has been claimed to be frequent among murderers and other criminals. Owen (1972) has challenged this finding, arguing that no adequate study of the incidence in criminals and noncriminals has yet been conducted. The seven XYYs he studied were normal in aggression but a little intellectually handicapped.

Sane and insane murderers

The concept of sanity is a legal rather than a psychiatric idea. It involves questions about an individual's understanding of right and wrong and awareness of what he is doing at a specific time. An insane murderer is one who does not understand (even temporarily) that murder is wrong or who is not aware that he is harming another person or both. The psychiatric concept of psychosis is roughly parallel to the legal concept of insanity, but it does not include any criteria about knowledge of right and wrong. However, a diagnosis of psychosis, like a decision that a person is insane, may be based on lack of contact with reality and unconsciousness of what one is doing. Specific behaviors, like reports of hallucinations or delusions, also enter into the diagnosis of a psychotic state. A person may be psychotic but be judged sane, or he may be insane but not psychotic, as in the case of a non-psychotic woman who kills her newborn child and is judged to have been temporarily insane as a result of the stresses of childbirth.

Guttmacher (1960) noted that murderers diagnosed as psychotic differed considerably from non-psychotics. The psychotics were more likely to have been psychiatrically hospitalized previously, less likely to have a prior conviction for a serious criminal offense or assault, more likely to be amnesic for the murder act, less likely to have been drinking immediately prior to the crime, more likely to attempt suicide after the crime, and more likely to kill a close relative or intimate friend.

Gibbens (1958) compared a group of murderers who had been admitted to a psychiatric hospital at some point in their lives to an unselected group of murderers of the same mean age. About one-third of the hospitalized murderers became psychotic at the time of the crime, about one-third murdered after an apparent remission from psychiatric disturbance, and the remaining one-third developed the disturbance after the crime, suggesting that the crime might have been an early sign of the impending disturbance.

Disturbed murderers often have delusions after the crime, believing that the victim is still alive, that he (the murderer) was found not guilty, and so on. Gibbens found that bringing the disturbed murderer to trial and convicting him had no apparent effect on these delusions, as compared to those of disturbed murderers who were not deemed fit to stand trial. (Of course, the two groups may differ initially with regard to the severity of the psychiatric disturbance and so be noncomparable.)

Schilder (1936) reported that psychotic or psychopathic murderers were preoccupied with death after the murder. Death and murder were seen as punishments. The murderers with no psychotic trends showed no particular concern with death and had a matter-of-fact attitude; the possibility of their own death seemed remote.

The disturbed murderers studied by Gibbens did not commit violent murders (murders involving repeated blows, multiple methods, or other special violence) more frequently than the nondisturbed, but they did more often kill multiple victims and were more likely to kill innocent persons. The groups did not differ in their family relationship to their victims. With regard to motives, delusional motives were, as might be expected, more common in the disturbed murderers. More frequently the disturbed murderers thought that the victims were plotting against them or had similar delusions. The two groups did not differ in sex-violence motivated murders; in fact, there were slightly more of these in the nonhospitalized group. The groups did not differ in number or type of previous offenses, or in the use of alcohol at the time of the murder.

Schipkowensky (1968) reported that murder was rare during the manic phase of manic-depressive psychosis but was more common during the depressive phase. This was especially true for altruistic murder which is intended to spare the relative suffering after the murderer's suicide. Batt (1948) compared murderers diagnosed as depressive psychotics with a group of female murderers judged to be legally sane (all the cases were female, except for one male depressive). The groups did not differ significantly in age, although the depressives tended to be older. They also tended to have been married more often. The married depressives had all killed their own children (and other family members in some cases), while the married nondepressives killed children in only two-thirds of the cases.

The depressed murderers were much more likely to be suicidal at the time of the act. They also more frequently sought assistance after the murder, while the normal murderers most often carried on with their daily routine.

All the depressives had prior symptoms of mental disturbance, so the act of murder was not a precipitant of the psychosis.

Comparisons with other criminals

Cruvant and Waldrop (1952) compared people who were convicted of second degree murder with those convicted of manslaughter or first degree murder and admitted to a psychiatric hospital. The people who were convicted of manslaughter were older and less educated and had more organic brain disease. The first degree murderers had more previous mental hospital admissions and more psychoses.

Comparing murderers and burglars, Kahn (1959) found no differences in sex, religion, occupational level or stability, marital status or stability, education, or drinking at the time of the offense. The murderers were older, more often black or Spanish-American, had fewer previous arrests, and were more often judged insane. There were no differences in IQ, but the murderers were more rigid in thinking and less capable of abstraction than the burglars. Kahn felt that murderers were characterized by having the potential for impulsive breakthrough of rigidly controlled hostility and fewer resources for indirect expression of hostility.

VICTIM-MURDERER RELATIONSHIPS

All the evidence suggests that people are most often murdered by someone they know. Only a relatively small proportion of murders are committed upon strangers. In Wolfgang's study of murder in Philadelphia, only 12 percent of the murderers were strangers to their victims. Only 1 percent murdered innocent bystanders. Another 1 percent involved murders of policemen and felons. Thirteen percent of the murder victims were mere acquaintances of the murderers. The vast majority, 73 percent, involved close friends, relatives, paramours of the victim or the murderer, sexual rivals, or enemies. There was a tendency for the murderer not only to know his victim but to resemble him. Pokorny (1965) found that murderers and their victims in Houston tended to live near each other. Thirty-three percent lived at the same address. Only 19 percent lived more than two miles apart. Even if one excludes murders between husband and wife, 51 percent of the murderers and victims lived in the same census tract.

The murderers and their victims were most often of the same sex and race, according to the studies of Pokorny and of Garfinkel (1949). Garfinkel reported data on homicides from ten counties in North Carolina for 1930 to 1940. There were 673 instances of homicide and 821 murderers. Garfinkel found that, on the whole, offender and victim were of the same sex, as is shown in table 3.

TABLE 3

Sexes of murderers and victims

	Murderer	Victim	Percentage	
	male	male	73.4%	
	male	female	14.6%	Same sex 76.9%
Sexes	female	male	8.5%	Different sex 23.1%
	female	female	3.5%	

Similarly, the offender and victim tended to be of the same race, as table 4 shows:

TABLE 4

Races of murderers and victims

	Murderer	Victim	Percentage	
	white	white	20.2%	
	white	nonwhite	2.9%	Same race 90.9%
Races	nonwhite	white	6.2%	Different race 9.1%
	nonwhite	nonwhite	70.7%	

THE ACT OF MURDER

Methods

Firearms and explosives are by far the most popular means of murder. Over half of the murders committed in the United States in 1964 involved those methods. Murder by cutting and piercing instruments came a poor second, amounting to only one-fifth of the murders. Another fifth involved "other means," which include beatings and strangulation. Table 5 shows the frequency of murder by various methods for the United States in 1964.

TABLE 5

Frequency of homicide methods
in United States*

Methods	Frequency to nearest percent
Poisoning	0.4%
Firearms and explosives	55.8%
Cutting and piercing instruments	21.5%
Other means	19.2%
Intervention of police	2.8%
Execution	0.2%

*Langberg (1967)

The use of cutting and piercing instruments was more common in the murders of nonwhites than of whites, whereas the use of "other means" was more common among whites. Also, females were killed by "other means" more than males but were less often killed by cutting and piercing instruments.

Wolfgang's study in Philadelphia found that black men tended to stab when they murdered, and to be stabbed or shot when they were the murder victims. White men beat and were beaten to death. Females of both racial groups most often stabbed their victims and were themselves stabbed or shot to death.

Wolfgang classified acts of homicide as to whether they involved one simple act of killing, or whether they involved multiple acts or a beating as well (violent homicides). He found that some 51 percent of all offenders committed violent homicides. Men were more likely to commit violent homicides than were females, but there were no age or racial differences. Female victims were more likely to be killed violently than male victims, but again there were no age or racial differences. Alcohol was present more often in the violent offenders.

Places

More murders occurred inside the home than out of it, in Wolfgang's study. Men killed and were killed most frequently in the street. Women were especially often killed in the home; they were most likely to be killed in the bedroom, but when they did the killing it was most likely to be in the kitchen.

MOTIVES WHICH PRECIPITATE MURDER

The study of the motivation of murder is a difficult one, but motives can sometimes be reconstructed by talking to witnesses and friends of the murderer and the victim. Questioning the murderer is also possible. One gets some answers this way, but their accuracy must be questioned to some extent. Not only may people lie, but they may be confused as to their own motivation. A man may feel that since he has killed, he must have had a specific motive—after all, murderers on television do. He may then examine his thoughts for ideas or problems which were preoccupying him just prior to the murder and choose one of them as his motive. Actually, the motive he chooses may have been irrelevant to the precipitation of the crime. Some trivial annoyance may have compounded general frustration and caused him to lose control of his aggressive impulses. Furthermore, he will not be aware of subconscious and unconscious motives for his act.

Nonetheless, questioning people after the fact is the best attempt made to establish motivation for a murder. Wolfgang found that murderers reported the motives shown in table 6 as precipitating the killing. Notably, one-third of all murders developed out of trivial arguments.

TABLE 6

Motives precipitating murder

Motive	Percentage*
Altercation over trivial matter	37%
Domestic quarrel	13%
Jealousy	11%

Altercation over money	10%
Robbery	8%
Revenge	5%
Accidental	4%
Hatred of victim	1%
Escaping arrest	1%
Concealing birth	1%

*Since some rare motives have not been listed, these proportions do not add up to 100%.

The influence of alcohol

Either the victim or the murderer or both had been drinking immediately before the killing in about two-thirds of the cases examined by Wolfgang. This was especially common in black victims and murderers. The relationship is not necessarily a causal one, though. Most of the murders took place on weekends when recreational drinking is more common than on weekdays. People of the same age, race, sex, and census tract who did not kill or get killed were probably also drinking at the time of the murders.

The time for murder

Wolfgang reported the fact that we have just mentioned, that murders are more frequent on weekends than on weekdays. Saturday night was the most dangerous time, according to his study. In the years 1948-52 in Philadelphia, there were a total of 380 homicides in the periods between 8 P.M. on Friday and midnight on Sunday, while during the rest of the week (about five days) there were only 208 homicides.

Nighttime is the most common time for murder. According to Wolfgang's study, more homicides occurred between 8 P.M. and 2 A.M. than at any other time of the day. This fact is supported by data from Houston (Pokorny, 1965).

Folklore has long supported the idea that the phase of the moon might be related to the occurrence of insane or deviant behavior. Pokorny (1964) examined data on homicides in Texas to see whether their occurrence was related to the phase of the moon. He investigated a total of 2,017 deaths (all of the homicides in Texas for the period 1959-61) and found no significant variation with the phase of the moon or with the apogee-perigee cycle.

Cerbus (1970) carried out a similar study in Ohio for the years 1962 to 1967. He found that deaths from homicide did not vary from month to month or from season to season (although total deaths, deaths from suicide, and admissions to mental hospitals did show a monthly and seasonal variation). Pokorny and Davis (1964) confirmed the lack of monthly and seasonal variation for homicides in Houston in 1960, and so did Wolfgang for Philadelphia in 1948-52.

Murder and other phenomena

In addition to lunar influences, magnetic effects like sunspot activity have been suggested as possible influences on the murder rate. However, Pokorny (1966) found that the deaths from homicide in Texas from 1959 to 1961 seemed to have no relationship to sunspot activity.

The earth's magnetic field also changes with time, and Pokorny and Mefferd (1966) investigated the possible relationship of geomagnetic changes to the homicide rate. They used several indices of magnetic storms but found no evidence of any association with acts of murder.

Pokorny and Davis (1964) examined homicides in Houston in 1960 to see whether there was any correlation between the time of the murders and the weather. They found no relationship for any of the weather variables that they examined: temperature, wind speed, wind direction, barometric pressure, relative humidity, visibility, ceiling height, rain, fog, thunderstorms, cloudiness, or the passage of cool northerly fronts.

We noted above that the homicide rate varied from region to region in the United States. D. Lester (1973) investigated whether the suicide rates of the different continental states varied systematically with their latitude and longitude. He found that the homicide rate increased significantly from the northern states to the southern states but that there was no east-west variation. (Suicide, by comparison, increases westward and northward.)

TAXONOMIES OF HOMICIDE

The first task of a science, many claim, is to classify and name the varieties of the subject matter under study: to devise a taxonomy. Although this may be true, frequently the resulting taxonomy is not used much in the study of a behavior. Much of the research conducted on murderers has merely used the dichotomy "murderer/nonmurderer," grouping all murderers together. An exception will be discussed later.

The fact that taxonomies are not used to any large extent in the study of homicide does not mean that no taxonomies have been proposed. Megargee (1969) has reviewed some of the major taxonomies, which we will describe here.

1. *Taxonomies of the   act.* One could easily form a taxonomy of murder by looking at the act itself. Categories could be based upon the method used, or, less usefully, the time at which the act took place or any other characteristic of the murder. We have used in this book an implied taxonomy based on the relationship between the murderer and the victim. This is shown in our chapter headings: husband-wife murders, parents who murder their children, and so on.

2. *Taxonomies of the motive.* Most psychological taxonomies are based on the motives behind the murder or the personality characteristics of the murderer. Buss (1961) has used the first classification to divide murders into two broad types: those in which the motive is to injure the victim and those in which the murder is a means to an end. Buss has called these types *angry aggression* and *instrumental aggression.* The two types can be illustrated by the parent who murders a child (see the case report in chapter 4) and a bank robber who kills some unknown bystander in his way. A more complex taxonomy of the motives for murder was suggested by Jesse (1952) who proposed six motives: killing for gain, revenge, elimination, jealousy, the lust of killing, and conviction.

3. *Taxonomies of personality differences.* Other taxonomies use the personalities of the murderers to arrive at a classification. For example, Megargee reports an unpublished taxonomy by John Conrad with six types: *(a)* the culturally violent, who live in a subculture in which violence is the norm; *(b)* the criminally violent, who kill in order to achieve some goal such as robbery; *(c)* the pathologically violent, who are emotionally disturbed; *(d)* the situationally violent, who murder

when extremely provoked, and *(f)* the institutionally violent, who are overly aggressive when incarcerated.

Banay (1952) described three types: *(a)* the subcultural murderer who is unable for some reason to adjust to societal rules; *(b)* the cultural murderer who kills in the course of robbery, to prevent arrest, or in gangland wars; and *(c)* the supercultural murderer, who is overinhibited and who has no outlet for his aggression until he explodes in one murderous act. The categories referred to by these rather odd terms resemble closely those of some of the other taxonomies we have discussed.

Glaser, Kenefick, and O'Leary (1968) provided another distinction: that between appropriate and inappropriate murders. Among appropriate murderers they included *(a)* the man who comes from a violent subculture, *(b)* the murderer who kills because of societal rules, as in socially prescribed revenge murders or the killing of clan enemies; and *(c)* the professional murderer or "contract killer." Among inappropriate murderers they included *(a)* the fringe individual who murders to bolster his self-esteem, *(b)* the brain-damaged person who lacks adequate impulse control, *(c)* the psychopathic murderer who lacks control over his aggressive impulses, and *(d)* the psychotic murderer. psychotic murderer.

Guttmacher (1960) divided murderers into these types: *(a)* the normal murderer, sane but with little regard for human life, *(b)* the sociopathic murderer, *(c)* the alcoholic murderer, *(d)* the schizophrenic murderer, *(e)* the temporarily psychotic murderer, *(f)* the symbolic suicide who kills another person in order to kill a part of himself which he has projected onto the victim, *(g)* the gynocidal murderer, who kills women as a defense against fears of castration, *(h)* the homosexual murderer who kills his lover, *(i)* the passive-aggressive murderer, and *(j)* the sadistic murderer.

Megargee (1966), the exception mentioned previously, has classified murderers as undercontrolled (people who habitually aggress beyond the social bounds, and who on one or more occasions lose all control of their anger and kill), or overcontrolled (people for whom anger is so inhibited that no mild expressions of rage are possible; under extreme provocation the anger breaks through and an exceptionally violent murder is committed).

This brief survey of taxonomies of murder indicates several things. First, there is little agreement among authors. Second, some of the terms chosen are distinctly odd (for example, the classification used by Banay and the broad dichotomy proposed by Glaser et al.). Third, the bases for the taxonomies are exceedingly varied. Guttmacher used primarily psychiatric diagnosis, Jesse used motives, and Conrad used a mixed basis. The attempt to work out a taxonomy of murder is probably useful primarily as a means of orienting research. Certainly no existing taxonomy can be said to describe any natural multiplicity of types of murderers.

Chapter 3

Law, psychology, and homicide

Several aspects of the legal treatment of homicide are important from the psychological and sociological points of view. First of all, the legal definition of homicide is important because of its contribution to statistical treatment of the topic. When it is said that fifty homicides have occurred, the killings referred to are only those which fit the legal definition; there may have been 100 other killings which the definition excludes. Second, knowledge of the legal definitions is necessary for comprehension of the process of convicting a murderer.

Related to the problem of definitions of homicide is the question of the insanity defense. Under what conditions is a killer not liable to the usual punishments for homicide? This brings up, too, the question whether the insane killer can be cured of his disturbance.

33

The legal aspect of punishment is also of interest, particularly with respect to the death penalty. In addition to inquiring if the death penalty is a deterrent to murder, one must ask whether or not the existence of a mandatory death penalty decreases the likelihood that the guilty will be convicted.

A final question about legal aspects of homicide involves the role of evidence in conviction. We will discuss some assumptions the law makes about the giving of evidence and point out that the assumptions are not always correct.

DEFINITIONS

The question of legal problems related to homicide leads into the rather turbid waters of definition. Legal definitions of homicide tend to use expressions whose meaning "everybody knows"—in other words, which no one can define in such a way that all other English-speaking people will agree with him. This raises a particular problem when legal definitions contain, as they often do, the concept of intentionality. The psychologist will consider it obvious, the nonpsychologist amazing, that modern psychology rarely attempts to deal with the problems of will, intention, or volition. The psychology of the eighteenth century, the time when present legal codes were developing, considered the will one of the basic factors of human personality. Thus, when modern psychologists try to deal with legal definitions of homicide, they find themselves faced with an integral concept which, though familiar to their predecessors, is quite foreign to them.

A second problem in the understanding of legal

definitions involves the use of words and ideas which must have very different meanings in different times and places. "Cruelty," for instance, meant something quite different to the slaveholder of the eighteenth century than it means to the educated man of today.

These difficulties should be kept in mind during the following discussion of the ways in which homicide is defined.

Homicide is the killing of one person by another and consists of several categories (Hoffman, 1952, quoted by Wolfgang, 1967).

1. *Excusable homicide* is an unintentional killing for which no blame attaches to the killer. It may result from negligence on the part of the victim. If the killer has been negligent, the act is termed involuntary manslaughter.

2. *Justifiable homicide* is an intentional killing sanctioned by law, as when a law officer kills a felon who resists arrest or when the officer kills in self-defense.

3. *Murder* consists of unlawful killing of a person with malice aforethought. Malice is a legal term which includes the elements of ill will, wickedness of disposition, hardness of heart, cruelty, recklessness of consequences, or a mind regardless of social duty. *(a) First degree murder* is the willful, deliberate, and premeditated killing of a person, feloniously and maliciously. Some codes include particular kinds of killing as first degree murder. In Pennsylvania, death resulting from acts of sabotage or from malicious injury to railroads is first degree murder. *(b) Second degree murder* is the killing of a person feloniously and maliciously but without intent to take life.

4. *Voluntary manslaughter* is the unlawful killing of a person in sudden heat of anger, without premeditation, malice, or depravity of heart.

5. *Involuntary manslaughter* consists of the killing of another without malice and unintentionally, but while doing some unlawful act not amounting to a felony or naturally tending to cause death, or in negligently doing some act lawful in itself, or by the negligent omission of a legal duty.

If the death of the victim does not take place within one year and one day of the assault, charges of murder cannot be brought. Charges of manslaughter are possible, however.

If a killing occurs while a felony is being committed, special rules apply. Any homicide which is committed while perpetrating or attempting a felony is murder. The death must be shown to have occurred as a consequence of the felony. It is not necessary for the killing to have been intentional or even for the act which caused death to have been intended. The felony in question must be a crime distinct from the act of killing. Thus, homicide while fleeing from a burglary is murder. Any killing committed in the perpetration of arson, rape, robbery, burglary, or kidnapping is murder. If one of a group of felons kills while engaged in a felony, then all the felons are guilty of murder, the principal offender being guilty of murder in the first degree and the accomplices of murder in the second degree.

In order to reduce murder to manslaughter in cases in which the victim played a role in the provocation of his own death, the following four prerequisites must apply: *(a)* there must have been adequate provocation; *(b)* the killing must have been in the heat of passion;

(c) the killing must have followed the provocation before there had been a reasonable time for passion to cool; and *(d)* a causal connection must exist between the provocation, the heat of passion, and the homicidal act.

Davidson (1946) noted that the states differ in their legal definitions of murder. New York considers murder in the first degree to involve a deliberate and premeditated design to kill the person (or to be the result of an act which is unpremeditated but imminently dangerous to others, or to be performed by someone engaged in committing a felony). In other states, such as Alabama, the killing must be malicious as well as deliberate and premeditated (which seems to imply that euthanasia would not be considered murder). Delaware requires that there be express malice aforethought, and other states refer to a "depraved and malignant heart." Davidson noted that the terms mentioned above included two concepts: will and emotion. The affective aspect of the definition is archaic and perhaps of little use. Will is the crucial factor.

The confusion of the law with respect to the "will" aspect of murder is illustrated by the New York penal law, which defines second degree murder as an act with design to kill but without deliberation and premeditation. Davidson noted that, as far as he could see, design without deliberation and premeditation is impossible.

HOMICIDE BY POLICE OFFICERS

Noncriminal homicide can be divided into two categories. *Excusable homicide,* in which the killing is unintentional, occurs without intent to harm and without criminal negligence, or when self-defense is necessary. *Justifiable homicide,* on the other hand, is an intentional killing, commanded or authorized by law, as in war, executions, lawful self-defense, or the process of arresting a felon.

In the United States, from 1950 to 1960, some 240 justifiable homicides by police were reported each year, a rate of 0.15 per 100,000 per year (Robin, 1963). Negroes are much more likely than whites to be killed (about seven to one nationally) by this means. Almost all (some 99.6 percent) of the victims are males.) Generally, the victims are young (half are below age twenty-eight), unskilled workers, killed between 9 P.M. and 9 A. M., typically on the highway, and die before reaching hospital of gunshot wounds. In a small sample of victims in Philadelphia, the majority of victims were being questioned about burglary, robbery, larceny, and assault. Most were reported to have resisted arrest. Almost without exception, the victims were said to have been warned of the possible fatal consequences of refusal to surrender (either verbally or by shooting into the air). About 75 percent of the small sample had previous criminal records and some 20 percent were judged to have had possible psychiatric disturbance.

The chance that a police officer will kill a felon varies quite widely from city to city; in Boston the annual rate per 100,000 police officers is 10.5 while in Akron it is 485.0. Nationally the rate is 194.2. Incidentally, some fifty policemen are killed in the line of duty each year, or about 31.7 per 100,000 police officers each year. Thus, policemen are about six times as likely to kill as to be killed in the course of their duty. The risk of death for policemen is about the same as for transportation workers.

THE "INSANITY DEFENSE" AND
THE PSYCHOTIC KILLER

The law has traditionally recognized that not all criminals are equally able to control their actions. There have been times, of course, when guilt rather than responsibility was the criterion for punishment—in eighteenth century England, for example, a child could be hanged for stealing some trivial object. In modern times, the law may consider guilty but does not necessarily punish the very young, the mentally retarded, and the emotionally disturbed. Particular legal problems have revolved around defining and identifying the last group.

Most legal thinking about psychotic murderers in the last 100 years has been based on the McNaghten rule, framed in the case of the murder of Robert Peel's private secretary. The McNaghten rule states, essentially, that a killer is legally responsible only if he knew at the time of the killing that his act was morally and legally wrong. He must also have known what he was doing, in other words have had criminal intent (*mens rea*). Following the McNaghten case, the House of Lords sought the judge's guidance on the subject of insanity and crime. The McNaghten rule, which is still in use in some states today, stressed that a person was presumed to possess sufficient degree of reason to be responsible for his crimes until it was proved to the satisfaction of a jury that the situation was probably otherwise. The defense had to prove that the accused was suffering from such a defect of reason, as a result of disease of the mind, that he did not know the nature and quality of his action, or, if he did know that much, that he did not know it was wrong.

Recent times have seen the phrase "disease of the mind" interpreted in differing ways. In England, in the last fifteen years, a number of developments have taken place. First, the concept of diminished responsibility was introduced—a term that covers the ground between legal sanity and legal insanity. Thus, judges are now able to apply a number of possible sentences rather than being confined to two extremes. Second, the definition of "abnormality of mind" was broadened. It now includes psychiatric disturbances and mental deficiency as well as temporary states of emotional disturbance such as the psychological trauma a man would experience in discovering that his wife had been unfaithful. Stress has also been acknowledged as a possible source of lack of emotional control, and the crime passionnel has been recognized (*Regina v. Fantle,* 1958).

The insanity defense is used to argue not that a killer did not commit an act but rather that he should not be liable to the usual penalties. This defense simultaneously makes it possible for the state to confine a person who is not legally responsible for his acts and who may be dangerous to the community, since the verdict "not guilty by reason of insanity" carries with it the possibility of long-term psychiatric hospitalization.

Curiously, the commission of a bizarre crime is not in itself proof of insanity. This is because the defense, which aims at saving the prisoner from serious punishment, would have to concede that he had committed the crime in order to use it as evidence that he was insane.

The use of the insanity defense has been questioned by Goldstein and Katz (1963, quoted by

Wolfgang, 1967). They noted that no legislative, judicial, or scholarly report has attempted to define the purpose of the defense. A commission appointed by the governor of New York in 1958 to improve the defense of insanity concluded that:

> we are unanimously of the view that there are compelling practical, ethical, and religious reasons for maintaining the insanity defense; . . . We believe . . . that it is entirely feasible to cast a formulation which . . . will sufficiently improve the statute to meet working standards of good morals, good science, and good law. [Report of the Governor's Committee on the Defense of Insanity, 1958, p. 4].

Goldstein and Katz noted that the report does not identify the reasons labeled practical, ethical, or religious, or the standards labeled good morals, good science, and good law.

Goldstein and Katz felt that the purpose of the insanity defense is to enable the state to confine and hold a person who has killed another even though he does not possess the guilty mind (*mens rea*). The insanity defense is not intended to define an exception to criminal liability, but rather to select for restraint a group of persons from among those who would otherwise be free of liability. Goldstein and Katz proposed tentatively that the insanity defense be abolished and *mens rea* made the requisite for criminal liability. The treatment of the mentally ill should be dealt with by a different set of laws.

We can add several comments here. First, the

absence of *mens rea* does not free the individual from all responsibility. The driver who runs over a pedestrian is liable, even though his act was inadvertent. He is convicted of manslaughter if found guilty. Analogously, it might be argued that a person who murders while insane (and thereby unaware of the consequences of his act, and so on) could be convicted of a lesser crime such as manslaughter.

Second, although the validity of Goldstein and Katz's criticisms of the present insanity defense is unarguable, the broader issue of responsibility must be raised. A large number of psychologists accept such concepts as the unconscious mind and such principles as determinism. Thinkers as different as Freud and Skinner have proposed that all behavior is determined by past experience and present stimulation. In so far as this is accepted, no murderer may be said to have acted voluntarily. In one way or another, his act was determined. Why, then, should insanity be the one concomitant factor that excuses a man's acts? Why not include a history of severe beating (which Palmer [1960] found to be related to subsequent tendencies to murder), or other relevant factors?

To argue thus is not necessarily to suggest that all murderers be found not guilty. The argument may as well be taken to mean that the insanity defense should be disallowed as an excuse for murder. What society does with its murderers can be decided on other grounds.

Davidson (1946) argued that any person who kills another and who is able to form a plan of action, as the act has shown him to be, is guilty of murder. A verdict such as "not guilty by reason of insanity" is improper.

The person is either guilty or not guilty. The proper question to ask about the insane murderer is what society should do with him. The treatment, whether psychiatric or juridical, and the aim, whether punitive or rehabilitative, is not relevant to the verdict. A man who cannot tell right from wrong or who does not know that murder is wrong is still a murderer if he has planned and executed a killing. He is guilty; what is done with him is another matter.

It might be argued that all murderers, despite the seriousness of their crime, deserve rehabilitative efforts, speedily applied, with release from prison when it is appropriate. At the other extreme, one might suggest that society cannot tolerate the presence in its midst of murderers, or the cost of keeping them on its fringes, so all murderers should immediately be executed. Probably, however, the best way of dealing with murderers lies between these two extremes and involves the tailoring of treatment to the killer. The tailoring of treatment should recognize the unique position of the insane murderer, a position which seems to differ from those of killers with abnormal genetic structures, abnormal EEGs, or pathogenic childhoods, but without present signs of emotional disturbance.

The application of the McNaghten rule, or any other rule requiring special treatment of the disturbed murderer, leads to a problem: what is the appropriate treatment of the person who is "criminally insane"?

An example of a psychotic killer was given by Robert Lindner (1954) in his well-known book, *The Fifty-Minute Hour.* The patient, whom Lindner treated briefly in a psychiatric hospital, had attacked a young girl who came to his apartment selling religious books. He invited her in, saying that his mother was in the back of the apartment. He then killed her with multiple stabs of an ice pick. After her death, he brought himself to orgasm by friction between her thighs and then tore her vagina with his fingers. He reported afterward that a voice had told him to kill. Later, in the hospital, after weeks of apparent normality, he went through a similar episode in which he tried to strangle Lindner, shrieking "Kill! Kill! Kill!" He was soon transferred to another hospital, since the authorities felt he was too dangerous to remain where he was, and Lindner lost track of him. The end of his story is not known.

What is the appropriate treatment for such a man? Can anything be done? Ordinary imprisonment will simply hold him in a relatively protected situation. We are sorry to have to say that confinement in most psychiatric hospitals will do no more. Perhaps intensive treatment by an excellent therapist could bring about a cure; it is difficult to say, for few such cases have ever received careful treatment. But the fact, from a practical point of view, is that such a man as Lindner's case is unlikely to receive much in the way of psychotherapy if he is committed to a state psychiatric hospital. The staff load in most such places is so heavy that a patient receives little in the way of professional therapeutic care. If he behaves badly and is difficult to deal with, he is likely to end up sedated on a chronic ward for the rest of his life. The choice between that and imprisonment, from a therapeutic point of view, is no choice at all. Those who have seen the film "Titicut Follies" will understand what we mean. As Szasz (1969) has pointed out, we take away more of a person's civil rights by declaring him emotionally disturbed than by convicting him as a common criminal.

What would happen if the murderer were sent to a good private hospital? This rarely happens since the state is not about to pay the high fees of private psychiatric treatment. If the killer came from a wealthy family, he would probably receive good care since the family would be able to pay for the intensive therapy which would rehabilitate him. However, it is our guess that people who come from wealthy families probably are seldom exposed to the kinds of experiences which make murderers.

In past years, a form of psychosurgery called prefrontal lobotomy was often used to calm excited patients. Prefrontal lobotomy is now rarely performed in this country, but neurosurgeons are experimenting with new psychosurgical methods aimed specifically at the control of aggression. These techniques attempt to control the functioning of the limbic area of the brain, which is thought to be responsible for aggressive behavior. Perhaps limbic surgery is a hope for partial rehabilitation of psychotic killers. It could at least convert them to peaceful psychotics. However, at this point its effect is not well enough documented to be considered a real solution to the problem. One must remember that prefrontal lobotomy, in its day, was hailed as the answer to many problems of mental illness.

Given that the prognosis for the psychotic killer seems to be a living death in prison or hospital, would society do best simply to put these people to death in a humane way? The reader will have his own opinion. Such a solution is not likely to be used in the foreseeable future, in any case.

CONVICTION AND PUNISHMENT

The principal question with respect to the murderer's punishment deals with the death penalty. Capital punishment, of course, used to be common for all sorts of crimes, ranging from murder down to trivial thefts. In the course of time, however, public opinion has turned against the death penalty, and the crimes for which it is used have gradually become restricted to serious ones. Today, there is considerable opposition to capital punishment even for murder, and many countries and states have abolished it. There are, nonetheless, a number of places where death is the mandatory or optional punishment for murder. Many people who live in places which have abolished the death penalty would prefer for it to be reinstated.

A major point which has been argued with reference to the death penalty is the possible deterrent effect of capital punishment—the idea that a murder is less likely when the potential killer knows that he may die as a result of killing someone else. There is no evidence that this is true (Schuessler, 1952). The murder rates stay the same in states which abolish the death penalty. Nonetheless, there is a widespread belief in the deterrent effect of the death penalty, particularly among policemen, who tend to predict massive increases in crime when abolition of capital punishment is proposed.

In addition to the deterrence argument, those who favor the death penalty sometimes feel that it is appropriate for society to exact vengeance for crimes, or that religious laws recommend execution in particular cases. They may argue, too, that noncriminals should not be taxed to support a murderer in idleness for the rest of his life. A somewhat different argument in favor of capital punishment suggests that death is actually a kinder alternative than life imprisonment, which confines a man in conditions of constant degradation and deprivation until death releases him.

Those who oppose the death penalty are sometimes concerned with the possibility of error, of the execution of an innocent man, which unquestionably has occurred on a number of occasions. They argue, too, that rehabilitation of the murderer is possible, and that execution negates the possibility that the killer can ever be useful and productive. Similarly, opponents of capital punishment point to the fact that few murderers ever kill again. There is also the argument that society is brutalized by its performance of legalized murder in the form of execution.

The facts about the deterrence argument are on the side of those who oppose capital punishment. The other arguments which we have summarized are based largely on value judgments and cannot be turned into testable hypotheses. For this reason, one's stand on the death penalty tends to be determined largely by emotional factors.

We might suggest, as others have done, that an effective deterrent punishment need not necessarily be severe, but it must be quick and sure. Under present circumstances, a murderer will not necessarily be caught, he will not necessarily be convicted if he is caught, and, even if he is convicted and sentenced to death, appeals and stays of execution may delay the actual punishment for years. The principles of learning theory show that punishment, if it is to be effective at all, must come close to the unwanted act. The most effective technique would be to punish just as the unwanted activity begins. The present punitive techniques are so far from this ideal that one can fairly say that the deterrent effects of legal punishments have never received an appropriate test.

Even if capital punishment were to be abandoned for the purposes of deterrence and vengeance, there would still remain the question of its use for one more purpose. There are, along with the many murderers who will never repeat their offense, a number who will kill repeatedly. Generally, these people are too disturbed to be deterred by any consideration of future punishment. The death penalty could serve the purpose of protecting society by permanently removing these rare individuals.

A final question may be added to the moral, ethical, and aesthetic considerations raised by the death penalty. The legal process itself may be affected by the existence of capital punishment, especially when it is obligatory after conviction for certain crimes. Juries may well be less willing to convict when their conviction is certain to mean death for the accused. If they have lingering doubts about a defendant's guilt, they will be aware that evidence coming to light in succeeding years will be of little help to him if the death penalty has already been applied. When the sentence is imprisonment, it may be easier for the jury to decide that guilt exists beyond a reasonable doubt. If one is concerned with procuring certain punishment for the murderer, then, this possible effect of a mandatory death penalty is an important consideration.

PSYCHOLOGICAL CONSIDERATIONS: EVIDENCE

The victim of a murderer is not in a position to swear out a complaint or to identify his killer upon inquiry. For that reason, conviction for murder is peculiarly dependent upon the giving of evidence by people who witnessed relevant events. Unfortunately, the law seems to assume that witnesses are far more reliable than psychological research has shown them to be.

Witnesses are asked to tell what they saw or heard which seems to have a bearing on the crime. They are assumed to be reporting their sensory impressions, not to be making inferences about what they must have seen. Two critical points are important here. First, the study of human perception has shown that all perception involves inference. There is no such thing as direct sensory contact which allows awareness of the "true" object somewhere out there in the environment. Instead, perception is a circuitous process in which many small sensations, small activities in receptor cells, are interpreted by the brain in an attempt to decide what object is most likely to be causing the stimulation.

The reader may remember having clearly recognized a friend across the street, crossed over with a smile and a wave, and then felt acutely embarrassed as the person was suddenly equally clearly recognized as a stranger. The sensory input was much the same throughout, but some slight change after crossing the street caused a sudden flip-flop on the decision about the person's most probable identity. Before and after the person's crossing, his perception was equally clear and definite. Perceptions are rarely indefinite from a subjective point of view. But they may be quite inaccurate even while the observer feels he could swear to what he is seeing. The reason is that perception always depends to a great extent on the process of inference, which is greatly affected by memory and expectation. Thus no witness can actually tell what he saw independently of telling his inferences.

Second, even perceptions which are relatively accurate at the time of the event have a way of being distorted in the course of remembering. The psychologist Hugo Munsterberg (1923) was one of the first to demonstrate this. In the course of an ordinary psychology lecture, he arranged for two men to rush into the classroom, stage an altercation which included the sound of a gunshot, and run out again. The accounts later given by the students who observed this unexpected interruption were distorted in the extreme. James Marshall (1969) conducted a similar experiment by showing a movie to law students, police trainees, and a group of people who attended a settlement house. Marshall was struck not only by the inaccuracy of their reports, but also by the number (particularly of the police trainees) who reported seeing events which had never happened.

In the face of these facts, it appears that the law should develop some better way of getting at what a witness saw than asking him to give a coherent report. The pressure on a witness to tell his story without inconsistencies or inaccuracies forces him to make further inferences, to decide that he must have seen or could not have seen particular events. This is a good situation for the lawyer who wants to bend the story to support or convict the accused, but it is not good for approaching that ideal which humans can never reach, the truth about what happened.

part 2

Patterns
of murder

Chapter 4

Parents who murder children

their own

About one out of every twenty murders committed in the United States in 1966 was of a child killed by his own parents; that is, about 500 people murdered their children. Resnick (1969, 1970) has reviewed available knowledge about these murders. The data and case histories reported in this chapter are based on his reports.

*TERMINOLOGY AND
LEGAL CONSIDERATIONS*

Infanticide refers to murder of a child by any person, related to him or otherwise. When a parent murders his own child, the act is called *filicide*. Resnick felt that murder of a child before it is twenty-four hours old is a different kind of behavior from filicide, and he called such an act *neonaticide.*

Filicide is unambiguously judged to be murder. Fathers who commit filicide are likely to be executed or sent to prison, whereas mothers who kill their children are likely to be hospitalized. Neonaticide is a more complex problem. Roman law recognized a father's right to kill his children, but in seventeenth century English law, an illegitimate newborn found dead was presumed to have been murdered by its mother unless witnesses said otherwise. By the nineteenth century, the parent was presumed innocent unless proved guilty, as in the case of other crimes. Several European countries today provide lesser sentences for neonaticide than for filicide, but only for mothers. The mothers are often charged with manslaughter while fathers who kill newborns are charged with murder. It is assumed that the mother's mind is disturbed from the effect of giving birth.

However, for a parent to be convicted of neonaticide, the baby must have been born prior to the murder. If it is killed while being born, before it breathes, then no murder has been committed. The difficulty of proving that the child had breathed and become a viable separate individual is often so great that the murdering parent is charged with concealment of the birth rather than with murder.

Mothers who commit neonaticide are often given reduced sentences, resulting in their being placed on probation only. Hospitalization is less common after neonaticide than after filicide, reflecting the reduced incidence of psychosis in neonaticidal mothers.

FILICIDE

Of persons who had killed their own children and who were studied by Resnick, 78 percent killed children who were older than twenty-four hours. The ages of the murdered children ranged from a few days to twenty years. Almost 30 percent of the children killed were under six months of age. Resnick suggested that this preponderance of young infants occurred because of the frequency of postpartum depression and psychosis within the period after birth and because the mother may consider the small baby as a personal possession. In the case of murders of older children, the children were more likely to be defective. The victims were equally divided between the two sexes.

The murders were twice as frequently committed by mothers as by fathers. The filicidal mothers ranged in age from twenty to fifty years, while the fathers were generally between twenty-five and thirty-five. About 60 percent of the filicidal parents were later judged to be psychotic. A diagnosis of depression was about twice as common for the murdering mothers as for the murdering fathers.

The method used in the murder tended to depend on the sex of the murdering parent. The fathers used active methods like striking, squeezing, or stabbing, while the mothers used drowning, suffocation, and gassing more frequently. There were a number of bizarre methods among Resnick's sample of murderers. One parent bit the child to death, while another put the child on a drill press and drilled a hole through his heart.

The motivation behind filicide is probably more complex and more varied than that behind ordinary

My studies have led me to fi...

murders of unrelated adults. Resnick described five motives which had moved the murderers he studied to commit filicide.

1. *Altruistic filicide* is performed with the object of preventing the child from suffering. Love and pity for the child lead the parent to kill in order to spare the child the pain which the parent expects for him should his life continue. Altruistic filicide may occur with the intention of relieving suffering which is already taking place (whether in reality or in the parent's imagination), or it may precede the suicide of the parent. In that case, the aim is to prevent the suffering which the child would experience when left alone after the parent's suicide.

2. *Unwanted child filicide* may *occurs when the c...* occur for several reasons. The child may be illegitimate or the offspring of an extramarital affair. Even a legitimate child may be seen as standing in the way of the parents' aspirations and desires. If the parents are immature, the infant may be seen as an intruder who gets in the way of their romantic involvement with each other.

3. *Spouse revenge filicide* may occur in a deliberate attempt to make the spouse suffer by depriving him of a favorite child.

4. *Accidental filicide* is the extreme form of the battered child syndrome. The parent may intend only to punish or discipline the child, but through over-zealousness or through accident (for example, the child falls downstairs when pushed rather than landing on the floor), the incident ends with the child's death.

5. *Acutely psychotic filicide* is a term used to describe killings when the parent is mentally disturbed. It is really a catchall category which contains all the

cases in which no other motive was apparent. The murder may be committed during a state of delirium in which the parent is not aware of his wild actions or their consequences, under the influence of hallucinations which frighten the parent or order him to kill, or in certain epileptic conditions in which loss of contact with reality occurs.

Following the murder of a child, the parent's behavior depends partly on his motive for the killing. The parent who has killed an unwanted child or the one who has killed the child accidentally may try to conceal what has happened. In the case of an altruistic filicide or of a psychotic one, however, the parent often seems dazed. He may confess mechanically or he may equally mechanically deny his act in spite of confrontation with the evidence. These parents usually do not try to conceal the murder or get rid of the body; instead they seek help.

A case of filicide: Mrs. Rogers

When Mrs. Rogers was twenty-nine and her fourth child was born, she began to feel tense and inadequate as a mother. She got some relief from these unpleasant feelings by spending time away from home and having two extramarital affairs. When Mrs. Rogers was thirty-one, she moved with her husband, a military pilot, to Alaska. Within a short time, her sleep pattern became more disturbed. Her increased irritability and depression culminated in a suicide attempt using an overdose of tranquilizers. When hospitalized, she acted contrite and was released after one week, although she remained in psychiatric treatment.

After her release from the hospital, Mrs. Rogers

remained apparently disturbed. She misinterpreted some of her psychiatrist's remarks and believed he had said that she should kill herself. When she told her husband that she needed help, however, he replied that neither he nor the children wanted her and that she should go away. In addition to the difficulty with her husband, Mrs. Rogers was concerned about her children. She felt that they were being raised materialistically. She was especially concerned that her second-born child, a five-year-old daughter, was a ruined "monster."

Within three months of the family's arrival in Alaska, Mrs. Rogers again decided to kill herself, this time using a car. However, she felt that her daughter would not be able to get along without her and took her along. She drove off a cliff and injured both herself and the child. The daughter's head was broken open, and the mother thought that now she had indeed made a "monster" of the child. Consequently, she killed the child by beating her on a rock. Mrs. Rogers then tried to kill herself by striking herself on the head, cutting her wrists, and throwing herself down the mountain. When these methods were not successful, she decided that her daughter should have a funeral. She climbed back up the mountain, where she was found thirty-six hours later.

Mrs. Rogers' family background had not been a healthy one. She remembered her mother as a materialistic, pretentious woman who was often away from home and to whom she had rarely been able to express her anger. The father, though kind, was weak and childish. He was later diagnosed as a paranoid schizophrenic. Mrs. Rogers' inadequate emotional capacity showed up after her marriage at the age of twenty-two. She was frigid and felt that her sexual inhibitions destroyed her husband's masculinity. Her feelings toward her parents, especially her mother, were acted out in her relationship with her children. The daughter whom Mrs. Rogers killed reminded her of her own mother and of herself as a child. She loved the daughter "more than anything else in the world" and felt as if she were punishing herself when she punished the child.

Resnick noted that the suicidal mother often sees her child as an extension of herself. This appears to have been the case with Mrs. Rogers and to have provided an important motive for the filicide. Mrs. Rogers projected her own feelings of unworthiness onto the daughter when she saw her as a "monster." Destroying the daughter was in a sense equivalent to destroying herself. The daughter was simultaneously seen as deserving pity because she was going to suffer from being motherless. Mrs. Rogers wanted to prevent the suffering. In doing so she was not only protecting the daughter but going through the motions of caring for her own childhood self, who was figuratively motherless because of her own mother's behavior.

In many cases of filicide, the aggression directed toward the child is a displacement of anger felt toward the murderer's parents, spouse, or sibling. Mrs. Rogers had felt abandoned by and angry toward her own mother. Her feelings of being abandoned were probably exacerbated by her husband's rejection of her after her affairs and her suicide attempt. By identifying the daughter with her own mother, Mrs. Rogers could express the anger her mother had never permitted. At the same time, by identifying the daughter with herself, she punished herself for daring to express anger. The filicide focused on the child the anger felt both toward the mother and toward the self, and in addition it brought in Mrs. Rogers' theme of abandonment concern as a rationalization of the desire to kill her daughter.

(Mrs. Rogers, incidentally, spent six months on an orthopedic ward recovering from her injuries and then four months on a psychiatric ward. She was then discharged to live with her family and a housekeeper. Mr. Rogers at first rejected her, apparently finding more difficulty in forgiving her infidelity than her filicide. Eventually, however, the marriage was resumed.)

NEONATICIDE

When Resnick (1970) examined a group of parents who had killed their newborn children, he felt that their acts were different from filicides. Nearly all of the neonaticidal parents were mothers, and they were significantly younger than the mothers who had killed older children. Some 90 percent of the parents who committed neonaticide were under twenty-five years of age. Depression and psychosis were less common among the neonaticides than among the filicides. Whereas about one-third of the filicidal mothers killed themselves, none of the neonaticidal mothers did so.

The most common reason for killing a newborn child was that it was unwanted, generally because it was illegitimate or the result of an extramarital affair. This motivation is rather different from the filicides where the most common reason for the killing was altruistic.

Most of the neonaticidal mothers were passive and immature. They had submitted to sexual advances rather than participating actively or initiating the relationship. On the whole, they did not have criminal records or a history of violent action. Instead the neonaticide was a desperate way to deal with a situation which they had made no plans to cope with. They made no attempt to have abortions and often denied the pregnancy or expected the baby to be stillborn. They prepared neither to care for the child nor to kill it. When the infant's first cry thrust reality upon them, they responded by silencing the intruder. The murdered child was usually their first-born.

In a few cases, the neonaticidal mothers were mature women who were intelligent, callous, and strong willed. They were older and more promiscuous than the women described earlier, and the crime was both premeditated and in keeping with their lifestyle. The motivation for these neonaticides, however, can surely not be simply getting rid of the child. If that were the case, one would expect the mothers to obtain abortions in some way rather than to go through with the birth and the problem of disposing of the infant's body. Some complex needs must have been involved in such murders.

A case of neonaticide: Mrs. Williams

The story of Mrs. Williams' neonaticide is a simple one, consistent with her passive, immature style of behavior at the time she became pregnant. While the history of a filicide generally is most involved with the events leading up to the murder, the case of this neonaticide is of most interest when one considers the events which followed the killing of the child.

Mrs. Williams dated her child's father a few times and passively allowed sexual relations because she wanted him to approve of her. When she found she was pregnant she resolved that her mother, with whom she was living, would not find out. She corsetted herself and was able to conceal her condition. She gave birth to the child at home, when no one else was there, and strangled it. The next day, she threw the body in the garbage. She was never found out and was amazed at her own coolness.

Since the neonaticide, Mrs. Williams' life has concentrated on evening things up—essentially, punishing herself in order to compensate for the murder. She had an affair with a drug addict which continued until he was jailed. She then became involved with a married man who finally married her. Mrs. Williams felt it would be appropriate for her to die in childbirth, but she did not become pregnant again. When she was thirty-six, a crisis developed after her discovery that her husband had been unfaithful. She stopped eating and lost twenty-two pounds in the next four months. Insomnia and indecisiveness forced her to stop her work as a secretary. She began to feel that others could read her mind and influence her through voodoo, and she dreamed that she and her husband were beaten, crucified, and murdered. Feeling that she was evil and deserved to die, Mrs. Williams drank poison, but she survived after a colon-esophageal transplant.

Mrs. Williams' family background and childhood experiences were not appropriate for the production of a mature, capable adult. As a child, she constantly sought her mother's approval but never felt that she got it. The parents slept in different bedrooms and separated when Mrs. Williams was fifteen. Nevertheless, the father continued to return to the house for the purpose of having Mrs. Williams wash his clothes. This family situation was ideal for the development of a passively promiscuous daughter. Mrs. Williams felt deprived of warm maternal affection. It would be natural for the child in such a case to turn her attentions toward the father in the hope of finding love. In most families, any sexual interest which might be aroused in the daughter by her unusual yearning for paternal affection would be to some extent inhibited by the knowledge that the parents were sexual partners. Mrs. Williams, however, was undoubtedly aware that her parents were sexually estranged. The father apparently treated her to some extent like a "junior wife," for example, by calling on her to perform the relatively intimate service of doing his laundry. There is no evidence that any incestuous relationship existed; however, the family situation might well arouse sexual interests that Mrs. Williams would then act out with partners from outside the family. Resnick suggested that Mrs. Williams' later concealment of her pregnancy from her mother resulted from the unconscious belief that the mother would consider it proof of incest. Mrs. Williams' sexual involvement would provide her with physical contact which would to some extent make up for the "mothering" attentions which she missed as a child. The fact that her contact was with a man would provide some satisfaction of the incestuous desires for her father which had developed as a result of her basic deprivation of parental affection. Her primary motivation in sexual relations was undoubtedly a matter of seeking emotional gratification rather than satisfaction of mature, genital sexual desire.

Resnick felt that Mrs. Williams' psychosis was a result of the neonaticide. She felt murderous impulses toward her husband after finding that he had been unfaithful, but she was unable to face these at a conscious level, perhaps because they suggested her previous murder. Instead, a psychotic process reversed the genuine aggressive desires into fears that she and her husband would be killed. By becoming psychotic, she was spared the reminder of the neonaticide for which she had been trying for so long to compensate. Two parts of her psychotic behavior are particularly indicative of preoccupation with the neonaticide. Her suicide attempt damaged her throat just as her baby's throat had been damaged through strangulation. Secondly, her failure to eat caused her to lose twenty-two pounds—a reversal of the gain of about twenty-two pounds which occurs during pregnancy.

Rather than attributing the psychosis to the neonaticide, one might be more accurate to say that the illegitimate pregnancy, the neonaticide, and the psychosis were all products of Mrs. Williams' passive, immature, emotionally constricted personality. The pregnancy was essentially denied except for her successful efforts at concealment. (Medical care was not sought; there were no plans for an abortion.) Mrs. Williams' amazement at her own coolness in killing the child and disposing of the body suggests a really heroic denial of feelings. She apparently simply did not experience the fear and anguish which one might expect to accompany her actions, although she expressed them in her behavior for many years after the neonaticide. The same failure to be aware of or experience her feelings occurred during her marital crisis, but this time, rather than many years of acting out, the feelings were dealt with more immediately by psychosis. Perhaps, if her emotional energies had not been drained by years of coping with the emotional aftereffects of the neonaticide, she would have had the resources to cope nonpsychotically with her husband's infidelity. In that sense, it might be true that the neonaticide was a causal factor in the development of the psychosis.

A CULTURAL PERSPECTIVE FOR NEONATICIDE

Not all societies have considered neonaticide to be a criminal act. Stern (1948) noted that the foundation stone of a building is a symbolic representation of the ancient practice of ritually stabilizing buildings by enclosing children in the foundations. The Mohave Indians often killed half-breeds at birth, while in China female children were often killed because of the expense of their dowry upon marriage and their inability to transmit the family name. Neonaticides of those with congenital defects or of one of a set of twins were common in many societies.

The examples given above suggest that neonaticide had many functions: ritual, as in the foundation stone practice; eugenic, as in the killing of children of mixed ancestry or of the deformed; and economic, as in female infanticide or the killing of children the family could not support. Freeman (1971) has suggested that female infanticide among the Canadian Eskimos also carried the social function of asserting male dominance within the household since it was the decision of the father alone whether any infant should live or die.

The historical frequency of neonaticide may be reflected in the more tolerant judgments of neonaticide than of filicide in our culture.

DISCUSSION

In later chapters, we will discuss the idea that there are two basic types of murderers: the overcontrolled type, who rarely expresses anger but who suddenly blows up one day, completely loses control, and kills; and the undercontrolled murderer, who is habitually violent and kills in the course of one of his ordinary brawls or fits of temper. This distinction seems relevant to some, but not all, of parents who kill their own children. In the case of accidental filicide, the parent is probably an undercontrolled type who habitually beats the child. One day, some accident turns the ordinary beating into murder.

Although there is little empirical evidence on the subject, one might speculate that the altruistic filicide is committed by an overcontrolled person. Although the altruistic killing of a child might be the result of a premeditated, rational plan to save the child from suffering, there is also the possibility that the murder occurs as the result of a sudden loss of control on the part of the parent. That is, the parent may have considered for a long time the possibility of killing the child for its own good, but the actual murder may not be a result of making a rational decision. Instead, the parent, frustrated for many years by the need to care for a sick, deformed, retarded, or disturbed child, may suddenly lose control and commit a totally unplanned murder. This suggestion is validated to some extent by Resnick's evidence that the parent who has committed altruistic filicide appears dazed and seeks help at once. Such behavior is not what one might expect of a person who has carried out a premeditated altruistic murder, which could be performed in such a way that it might appear to be a natural death or an accident (for example, by an overdose of some medication usually given to the child). A person who could murder by cool premeditation might be expected to carry off the aftermath of the murder better than Resnick describes.

The act of neonaticide fits less well into the undercontrolled-overcontrolled dichotomy. Resnick's neonaticidal mothers do not seem to have been undercontrolled as far as aggression was concerned. They were passive, quiet people who had no police records. Nor does there seem to be real evidence to suggest overcontrol. The mothers do not seem to have responded to some irritating act of the infant's by losing control and killing it. Loss of control in a fit of rage seems especially unlikely in the state of physical and emotional fatigue which follows childbirth. Instead, we might suggest that neonaticide, rather than resulting from a disturbance of control over aggressive impulses, is the result of a general inability to cope maturely with life. The mothers who killed their newborn infants did not make preparations either to kill the baby or to take care of it. To a considerable extent, they simply ignored the fact of its imminent birth until labor was upon them. When the child was born, they responded to it in the way which required the least effort and the least planning— murder.

Chapter 5

Bang, bang, you're dead!

For a young child to kill—especially for him to kill an adult— is not easy, for murder requires a certain amount of physical strength, agility, and understanding of bodily processes. Nonetheless, some children do succeed in committing murder, in performing killings which are obviously not accidental.

Prior pathology in child murderers

Some researchers have felt that murders by children are simply extensions of the children's past behavior which showed evidence of disturbance. In a study of thirty-three child and adolescent killers by Bender (1959), most seemed to be impulsive and all but three had some pathology such as schizophrenia, brain disease, or epilepsy. Events in their past lives which could be seen as antecedents of the murders include compulsive fire setting, retardation in school, unfavorable home conditions, and personal experiences with violent death. Other investigators have found evidence of prior pathology like frequent bedwetting (Michaels, 1961) and abnormal dysrhythmia in the EEG (Woods, 1961). These investigators thus imply that child murderers have a tendency to irritability and poor impulse control which is to some extent biologically determined.

The adult as puppet-master

Another approach to murder by children suggests that the child killer acts as the unwitting agent of an adult (Sargent, 1962). The adult consciously wishes that some other person were "out of the way," but does not consciously seek his death or overtly instruct the child to kill him. Over a period of time, though, subtle indications from the influential adult communicate to the child that a murder would be greeted with approval. The child does not feel that he has been coerced into the murderous act, but willingly accepts responsibility for it. However, he is surprised that the victim is dead and says that he did not really mean to kill him. The child murderer tends to have a protective attitude toward the influential adult, which leads him to do what the person seems to want without really understanding the seriousness of his action. The victim is a person toward whom the child might well have felt some hostility in the normal course of events, but, without the subtle prompting of the other adult, the child could have controlled his aggressive feelings.

Sargent discussed the case of eight-year-old Art and his seven-year-old brother, who shot their father, an eccentric recluse. The father, who had been divorced from the mother for several years, believed that he was Jesus Christ. He wore old clothes and a beard and had predicted that he would die at the age of thirty-three and one-half (Jesus' age at his death). He also predicted that his death would come at the hands of his children.

Despite the boys' protests and her awareness of her husband's aberrations, the mother allowed the children to visit him during the summer vacations. During these trips, the father had the boys clean his cabin, prepare his meals, and submit to his whims. He beat them if they disobeyed.

On the day before the father's death, he forbade his sons to touch him or come near him. When one accidentally touched him, he threatened to beat them both. He ordered them outside and sat with his back to the door, reading the Bible. Art and his brother went to the car, removed the gun from the glove compartment, loaded it, and shot the father from a distance of thirty feet. The father was exactly thirty-three and one-half when he died.

The mother later said that if Art had not killed his father, she would have done so because she hated the man so much. She noted that Art's excellent marksmanship had been taught him by his father. Four years before the murder, when the boys were temporarily with their father, Art had asked his mother when they would be able to be with her all the time; she replied that that could happen only when the father was dead.

The mother's influence is evident in this case of murder by a child. She overtly admitted her desire for the victim's death. She told Art that he could count on being with her, the preferred parent, only when the father was dead. In addition, she encouraged the growing hostility Art felt for his father by sending the boys to be with the father when they did not want to go.

A curious feature of this child murder is the extent to which it was precipitated by the victim. The father prepared his death by instructing his rather young son in marksmanship and leaving a gun in easy reach. This, coupled with his prediction that he would die at the hand of his children, suggests that he achieved exactly what he wanted. He even appears to have set up the exact time of death by his strange behavior immediately preceding the murder. His refusal to be touched, the ultimate rejection of any affection the children might still feel for him, was in a sense permission for Art's anger to be mobilized. The father declared himself no longer a father to be loved, but instead an enemy whose only function was to keep the boys away from the mother they loved.

The child's situation

To understand the circumstances in which the murdering child finds himself, one must realize that a child's understanding of death is not the same as an adult's. The child often assumes that death is reversible, that it is simply a temporary punishment or deprivation. The playmate who is "killed" while playing cowboys soon gets up again. The murdering child is incredulous at the consequences of the real killing and cannot accept that his victim will never come back to life. This is particularly true because powerful rage is often present in children's lives, under perfectly normal circumstances; the child has already experienced the emotional situation in which killing could occur. Only when some compounding situation occurs, however, does the familiar anger become uncontrollable and result in an immutable death.

Bender and Curran (1940) suggested that the primary problem for children who murder is rivalry for the attention of a parent or foster parent. This alone is rarely expressed in murder. Certain complicating situations must be present in order for murder to result:

1. *Family rivalry may become unusually severe because of some external factor.* For instance, Clare was the first child of a drug-addicted father and an inadequate mother. The mother put Clare in a foster home when she was expecting her second child because she felt she could not cope with her at that time. Clare became jealous of the baby, whom people called "Shirley Temple." When the mother was expecting a third child, both the older children were sent to the same foster home. Clare fed the sister dirt, dropped her onto a stone walk, and tried to choke her, but the younger child survived.

2. *In a foster home situation, the child may have no strong positive feelings of love to curb the strong aggressive tendencies.* In a case of this kind, Roger came to the foster home from a difficult background. His father had died when he was two, and his inadequate mother had gone to live with a violent, irritable man by whom she had two more children. The stepfather hated Roger and frequently beat him while the mother stood by. The mother rarely visited Roger in the foster home, but two younger boys in the home were frequently visited by their mother. Roger tried to dominate the situation by being aggressive and finally tried to gas the younger boys.

3. *Organic inferiority makes the child feel helpless and in need of greater love, which he does not always receive.* John, for example, was a dwarf. His development halted when he was one and a half, which coincided with the birth of the next sibling. Two other children followed. All the younger children developed normally and received more of the mother's love. At the age of five John was trying to kill his siblings. He tried to push the babies off window sills and stuff objects down their throats. He said he hated his mother for having so many children and his brothers and sisters for taking his mother's attention.

4. *Insurmountable educational difficulties (due to reading disabilities or similar problems) may lead to marked feelings of inferiority in children who have the insight to sense their inferior status.* George had had a birth injury which left hemiparesis and a severe speech handicap. At twelve, he also had a reading disability. Making little progress in school, he reacted by playing truant and stealing. Around puberty he became more aggressive, stole openly, and became sadistic. After being admitted to a psychiatric ward, he tried to hit other patients on the head with chairs during his temper outbursts.

5. *When the parents are aggressive, the child tends to identify with them and to pattern his behavior after theirs.* The case of Roger, noted above, is probably a good example of this syndrome as well as of the foster home problem.

The adolescent murderer

Murder committed by an adolescent is more like the act of an adult than the act of a child. The adolescent understands the irreversibility of death and realizes the nature of his act. The fact that his victim is often a parent, however, shows that the adolescent, unlike most adults, is still much attached to his own family, on whom his greatest desires and fears are projected. One might say that adolescent murder combines the family rivalries and rages of childhood with the powerful sexual motivations of adolescence (including the struggle with incestuous desires) and the skills of adulthood.

Smith (1965) felt that many of the cases of adolescent murderers that he had seen fitted into the category of episodic dyscontrol suggested by Menninger and Mayman (1956). In the cases Smith reviewed, the early life had been marked by a disintegrated family relationship, and the child had had no positive and stable ego models to identify with. When stressed later, the weakened ego functions ruptured. In most cases it was a parent or parental symbol who was murdered. Often the victim was provocative, perhaps in a nagging, carping, or derogatory way.

A form of adolescent murder which has attracted much study is that of matricide. Murder of the mother is almost invariably carried out by a son, rather than a daughter. A theme of overt or covert incestuous involvement is common, with passions and anger rising as the son enters puberty.

Scherl and Mack (1966), who studied three cases of adolescent matricide, felt that the cases shared a history of severe early maternal restrictiveness with alternating deprivation, provocation, and harshness, extending into adolescence. The mother-child relationship was intense and conflict laden, ending in violent murder. The fathers were passive and relatively uninvolved in the mother-child interaction; they generally remarried within a year and a half of the murder.

A case of matricide

As an example of matricide, we will describe and discuss a case reported by Scherl and Mack. The killing took place when Gordon (as we shall call him) was not quite fifteen years old. His mother had become angry with him because he sold a present she had given him. As was the family custom, the father beat Gordon with a belt while he lay on his bed. The beating was severe, and the mother, who seems to have been somewhat upset, went out for a few hours. Gordon went to bed, later saying that he forgot all about the beating. The next morning, after the father had gone to work, the boy dressed, loaded his father's rifle, and killed his mother as she lay in bed. Gordon then changed his blood-splattered clothes and went to a local priest, to whom he confessed his act in an apparent state of confusion.

The relationship between Gordon and his mother had long been one of erotically tinged hostility. The mother rejected him from birth, and, in fact, he was cared for by an aunt for the first month of his life. Gordon felt that his mother always blamed him for his unattractive appearance as a newborn baby and for the trouble he caused her. The parents agreed to have no more children, but they did care for foster children in the course of Gordon's childhood.

Scherl and Mack described Gordon's early life in this way:

According to [Gordon's] description, his life within the family consisted from early childhood of persistent, but inconsistent rejections, beatings, and humiliations. The first misdeed he can recall was the theft of five pennies from his mother's change bank at age five, for which he was strapped. A year later he recalls being unjustly accused of the theft of a rake and an umbrella for which he was again punished. He states now that after this experience he concluded that if punishments were to be repeatedly forthcoming, he would commit acts which would at least justify such punishments. He recalls first hating his mother for a brief period at age seven when she falsely accused him of stealing a dime. For this, according to his account, he was made to kneel in a corner for some twelve hours. The father's only intervention upon returning home was to ask the boy whether he had stolen the dime, which he denied. [Gordon] also attributes to these early years the memory of an unconfirmed suspicion that his mother was entertaining another man when his father was away from home. By the time he was eight or nine, [Gordon] would deliberately and stubbornly allow himself to be punished rather than admit to misdeeds of which he claims he was in fact innocent. He recalls from this period a fight between mother and father over the type of windows to be installed in a house the family was building. The disagreement was so intense that the parents went separately to bed. The mother began to wail and eventually in [Gordon's] presence the

father attacked and began strangling her. [Gordon]
several times separated the parents. He cites this
story to prove it was impossible to win against
mother. . . . He speculates that he alone stood up
to her and that this was perhaps another reason she
hated him so. [Pp. 574-575]

Gordon's mother frequently felt he should be
punished physically, but she refused to carry out the
beating herself. She would get her husband to do it, or,
if he was not at home, call on a maternal aunt to beat
Gordon for her. Gordon's childhood was marked by
impulsive fighting and scholastic difficulties. At Gordon's puberty, his aggressive tendencies became more
marked. He had frequent fights in which he would lose
control and want to kill his opponent. There were
episodes in which his mother would kick, slap, and
swear at him, leading to even further resentment on
Gordon's part. There was one suicide gesture at this
time, when Gordon feared punishment following the
discovery that he had stolen some money.

Gordon first fantasied killing his mother in early
adolescence. He was angry about a punishment at the
time. Soon after, there was some erotic interaction
between the mother and a neighbor, which Gordon
observed. He felt angry and disgusted, as he did when
his mother was partly exposed while sitting down or
when wearing her housecoat. His powerful denial of
incestuous wishes toward his mother, shown in his
"disgust" at her, developed simultaneously with his
desire to kill her.

At the same time, he began to enjoy their frequent
fights. The erotic and hostile components of his feelings
toward his mother were becoming interwoven. This was

compounded by the fact that, a few months before the murder, he caught his mother in bed with the neighbor mentioned above. He never told the secret but would hint at it with his mother. His discovery must have furthered his erotic-hostile involvement with his mother. It gave him good grounds for jealousy and for resentment because she was unfaithful to his father, and also stressed the fact, which Gordon was struggling to deny, that the mother was a woman with whom it was possible to have sexual relations. To complicate further his confusion about his role as a male in the household, Gordon's father was encouraging him to have sexual relations with girl friends, even providing him with contraceptives—in a sense asking him to act out some of the things the father had always been too passive to do.

For several months before the homicide, Gordon was placed in a situation in which relations with the mother became more and more difficult. The father was often away. Gordon was working on a farm for the summer, and his mother insisted on taking most of his earnings to "save" for him. The mother became more and more nagging, intrusive, and provocative, refusing Gordon permission to go out. She started drinking and became so abusive that Gordon feared she would kill him. Gordon ran away at this time, was sent to a youth detention center for a while, and then was released. The parents were reprimanded by the court for their behavior. They were advised to let Gordon live away from home, but they never arranged to do so.

The beatings and nagging continued during the next few months. Scherl and Mack felt that Gordon almost deliberately provoked the final argument and beating, which "justified" him in killing his mother at last.

Adolescent matricide is evidently a more complicated event, psychologically speaking, than murder by a
child. The most important pathological component
seems to be the mother's provocation, combined with
her long-term manipulation of her son's erotic interest
in her. When puberty arrives and the son becomes
capable of active sexual interest, the mother must be
simultaneously jealous of his girl friends and frightened
by the possibility of overt incestuous relations. She does
not want to let the son go, but she cannot use her
sexuality to bind him closer. The result is anger and
resentment, shown in what one might call an intimacy
of hostility—the working off of passion in verbal battles
which both need and enjoy at some level. This may be a
safe solution from the mother's viewpoint, but it only
provides further stress for the son. He is distressed by
his "infidelity" to the mother when he is interested in
other women, but cannot accept his interest in her. The
anger resulting from this dilemma is compounded to the
point of loss of control by the mother's angry nagging
and belittlement.

If the father were an active family participant, he
could save the situation by encouraging the son to have
mature heterosexual and social interests and by support-
ing him in the face of the mother's criticism. Instead,
Gordon's father acted as an instrument of the mother's
wrath and was otherwise passive except for his attempts
to push Gordon into premature sexual activity for his
own vicarious pleasure.

Chapter 6

Till death
do us part

Murder begins at home in a large number of cases. Parents, children, brothers, sisters, and spouses are frequently a murderer's victims. He kills the people he is most involved with, rather than strangers or casual acquaintances.

Wolfgang (1956) conducted perhaps the most useful study on murder between spouses. His findings give us a picture of the general nature of husband-wife murders. In Philadelphia, the scene of Wolfgang's investigation, between 1948 and 1952, there were a total of 621 murderers and 588 dead victims. One hundred of the victims were spouses of their killers—fifty-three wives slain by their husbands and forty-seven husbands killed by their wives. Wives constituted 41 percent of all the women killed, whereas husbands constituted only 11 percent of all male victims. When a man was killed by a woman, the murderer was most often his wife. When a woman committed homicide, she was more likely to kill her mate than were male murderers; 45 percent of the female murderers killed their spouses, while only 12 percent of the male murderers did so. Eighty-three percent of the husbands murdered violently (that is, with several different acts of assault) whereas only 38 percent of the wives did so. In general, husband-wife slayings were more violent than other murders.   ✓

Eighty-five percent of the mate slayings occurred in the home, the majority of them in the bedroom. The bedroom was more lethal for wives; 45 percent of the wives and only 23 percent of the husbands were killed there. More husbands than wives were killed in the kitchen.

Wives usually stabbed their husbands, while husbands used most of the common methods in the proportion expected from the general population of murderers. Of husbands killed in the kitchen, most were stabbed with a kitchen knife, which Wolfgang felt indicated the impulsive nature of the act.

Mate slayings were more often victim-precipitated than were other murders (33 percent versus 26 percent). Husbands seemed to precipitate their own murders more than wives did. Wolfgang felt that this fact could have any one of several meanings. (1) Husbands may actually provoke their wives more often than vice versa, or (2) wives are more susceptible to provocation than are husbands and react more violently, or (3) husbands may have a greater sense of guilt for some reason and receive provocations without retaliating, as if they were being punished, or (4) husbands may withdraw from marital conflict more than wives and thus inhibit any responses they might make to their wives' provocation.

More husbands than wives were found guilty (64 percent versus 55 percent), while more of the wives were acquitted (34 percent versus 4 percent). More husbands committed suicide (19 percent versus 2 percent)—perhaps evidence of greater guilt because they had killed with less provocation. Husbands were convicted of more serious offenses than were wives. No wife was convicted of first degree murder, whereas first degree murder was the verdict for ten of the thirty-four men. This difference in the court's treatment may be a result of the greater incidence of victim-precipitated homicide when wives killed husbands.

Men who kill their wives.

To fill out Wolfgang's statistics, we turn now to a psychiatric investigation of twelve wife murderers (Kurland, Morgenstern, and Sheets, 1955). Nine of these twelve men were clearly psychotic, and a tenth developed a psychotic state soon after imprisonment.

The marriages, which seem to have been of relatively long duration, were characterized by a typical relationship between husband and wife. The wives did more than their share of family tasks and were dissatisfied but unable to leave the husband. There were occasional separations which did not last long. The husbands were domineering, "unstable, self-centered, jealous of their wives and offspring, and . . . becoming increasingly inadequate socioeconomically" (Kurland et al., p. 8). With respect to sexual relationships, the men were in especially bad trouble. They seemed to have deep and basic sexual fears which they had tried to deal with through the convention of marriage. (The wives were often frigid, incidentally.) However, the relationship with the wife had eventually reawakened this sexual anxiety. Some of the wives who survived the attack reported that the sexual relationship had become a subject of greater and greater indifference. The husbands had responded to this by becoming more anxious about their inadequacies and had attempted to exert their dominance (not only in the sexual sphere) by force. The husbands had always been suspicious of their wives' fidelity. Some even denied their own children.

Kurland and his colleagues felt that the basis of the men's difficulties was an inappropriate sexual identification. Rather than feeling clearly that they were men, as their own fathers had been, they were deeply involved at an unconscious level with some much feared female figure. Simultaneously, they identified themselves with the feared woman and used their wives to represent her. Kurland et al. described the results of this inappropriate identification:

> When the personality structure finally fractured, each one displayed a strong homosexual conflict suggesting the passive, unconsciously homosexual male who projected this attitude on his wife. When he finally reacted to a wave of overwhelming hostility, he murdered his wife rather than attack the suspected lover of his wife. It is also significant that each one felt that he loved his children and treated them as his own, although he believed they were not his. This is taken as evidence that his attitude is feminine-maternal and his wife is really regarded as a rival. [P. 9]

The precipitation of the murder apparently depended on the wife's behavior. Two special factors seem to have been important. First, the wife had a strong need to deny that she had been unsuccessful in establishing a happy family. Her husband served as a ready scapegoat; the worse he looked, the better the wife appeared. She sometimes managed to push the husband almost entirely out of the normal family interactions. In any case, she had reason to encourage him to act even worse than he might otherwise do.

A second factor was the wife's manipulation of guilt. Not only did the wives point out to their husbands how much they were suffering, but they also tried to keep their own behavior beyond reproach, so the husbands had little reason for realistic criticism. Simultaneously, as we noted above, the wives had reasons to give subtle encouragement to the behavior they overtly deplored. This mechanism gave the wives momentary satisfaction, but in the long run,

> It would appear that one of the most destructive forces in the priming of the ultimate explosion was the use of this guilt mechanism. By giving the husband less and less cause to be realistically critical, the wife was in turn causing him to become tormented by an increasing accumulation of unconscious guilts. With no means of communication to relieve the situation, he finally discharged in an overwhelming outburst of violence. [Kurland et al., p. 11]

The murdering woman

Women kill much less frequently than men. Generally speaking, they are not likely to kill anyone except their husbands or children. Since that is the case, we will take this opportunity to discuss some of the characteristics of women who kill.

Ward, Jackson, and Ward (1969) studied female offenders in California and compared the female murderers to the women imprisoned for other crimes. The female murderers were 65 percent white, 25 percent black, and 10 percent Chicana. They tended to be of average to below average intelligence, came from families which were unbroken and had no criminal record, and frequently had been sexually promiscuous or prostitutes. Many had serious drinking problems, but there were virtually no reports of narcotics use. Most of the women were diagnosed as emotionally disturbed.

Compared to the other women offenders, the murderers had the least extensive prior criminal record, the highest age when first arrested, the largest proportion of alcoholics, the smallest proportion of narcotics users, and the highest incidence of psychosis.

The act of murder most often took place at home, with a spouse, lover, or child as victim. It was unpremeditated and did not require much physical strength because the victim was either helpless (a child) or incapacitated (drunk or asleep).

Another group of investigators (Cole, Fisher, and Cole, 1968), who studied eleven women murderers, described six kinds of female killers.

1. *The masochistic woman murderer* is stable, with a good reputation, often religious, well controlled, reliable, and productively employed outside the home. She is married to an abusive, unstable mate. After years of abuse she commits a violent murder, often while being beaten or when fearful of being killed. After

killing the mate violently, she calls for help and exhibits some degree of shock. She expresses sorrow, loss, remorse, and depression.

2. *The overtly hostile type* is emotionally unstable, aggressive, and impulsive. She has been violent in the past and dislikes any authority or limitation. She attacks her victim with the intention of hurting, not killing. She shows a sense of loss if the victim was an intimate, but little guilt or depression.

3. *The covertly hostile type* is usually not a violent person, but she murders violently. Usually, she expresses hostility only when it is safe. These women often kill their children. Their mates are often hostile and abusive, but the wives are afraid to fight back. They are poor homemakers and mothers. Their interpersonal relationships are superficial, and they feel wronged and deluged by demands. They deny the offense at first, and show little remorse or sense of loss.

4. *The psychotic woman murderer* kills during a psychotic episode or after feeling an indiscriminate urge to kill for some time. These women are chronically disturbed, with poor interpersonal relationships, few goals, and flat affect. They do not recall the crime and feel no remorse.

5. *The amoral woman murderer* commits a deliberate and planned killing, for economic gain or to remove someone who is interfering in a heterosexual relationship. She has an asocial and antisocial record, often with past criminal activity. The amoral murderers have a high level of ability and functioning but lack awareness of the feelings of others, whom they treat as objects.

6. *The inadequate woman murderer* has little coping ability. She depends on a dominant lover,

husband, or friend, and takes on few commitments beyond the avoidance of stress and attempts to please the partner. Confusion, flattened affect, and limited intelligence are typical. Often such women have been ordered to act by the dominant partner.

Generally, then, women murderers do not seem to fit the undercontrolled and overcontrolled categories we have described for male murderers. Only the overtly hostile type described by Cole et al. seems to fit that dichotomy. Most of the women in the other categories have never been habitually violent. Overcontrolled women murderers are even less in evidence than habitually aggressive ones. Perhaps women in this culture are not subjected to the kinds of pressures which create the unnaturally "good" man who reacts to stresses by overwhelmingly violent actions.

Chapter 7

Presidential assassins

Attempts to bring about political change by murdering a leader have undoubtedly been made since long before history was recorded. The word *assassination*, however, is of comparatively modern date. It is derived from *Hashishin*, the name of a group of political murderers in the tenth and eleventh centuries in Iran who were users of the drug hashish (hemp). The Hashishin were a secret order of religious fanatics who spread their influence throughout northern Iran and Syria by building a chain of hill forts and pursuing a policy of assassination of their enemies. Their leader, the Shaykh-al-Jabal or Old Man of the Mountains, insured their loyalty and devotion to murder by providing them with hashish under the guise of a brief visit to Paradise. Most modern assassins, however, have needed neither social support nor drugs to motivate them, being driven quite sufficiently by their own inner needs.

The course of history abounds with famous assassinations—the political murder of Julius Caesar by Cassius and Brutus, the assassination of Marat by Charlotte Corday, the killing of the Archduke Franz Ferdinand of Austria, which helped to lead to the First World War. Unfortunately, little is known about the psychological nature of the assassins in these historical cases. In spite of their political and historical interest, they can give little help in an attempt to analyze the psychological nature of assassination.

The assassins about whom most is known are those who killed or attempted to kill presidents of the United States. The recency of the events and society's interest in them have helped to preserve a good deal of information about these people. There are also a large enough number of cases to make investigation worthwhile. Four presidents have been killed while in office (Lincoln, Garfield, McKinley, and Kennedy), two have been attacked but not injured (Jackson and Truman), and one president-elect was attacked but not wounded (F. D. Roosevelt) (see table 7). Theodore Roosevelt, while running for a second term, was also wounded by an assassin. Because of the relatively complete information available about the presidential assassins, we shall concentrate on them rather than on other political murderers.

Types of assassinations

Assassinations fall into three rough categories: murders by a hired killer who has no personal involve-

TABLE 7

Summary of actual and attempted presidential assassinations*

Assassin	Intended victim and date	Outcome
Richard Lawrence	Andrew Jackson January 30, 1835	Jackson not hurt. Lawrence committed to mental hospital until his death in 1861.
John Wilkes Booth	Abraham Lincoln April 14, 1865	Lincoln fatally wounded. Booth killed by self or soldier 12 days later.
Charles J. Guiteau	James A. Garfield July 2, 1881	Garfield fatally wounded. Guiteau hanged June 30, 1882.
Leon F. Czolgosz	William McKinley September 6, 1901	McKinley fatally wounded. Czolgosz electrocuted October 29, 1901.
John N. Schrank	Theodore Roosevelt October 14, 1912	Roosevelt was wounded. Schrank committed to mental hospital, died 1943.
Giuseppe Zangara	Franklin D. Roosevelt February 15, 1933	Roosevelt not hurt. Mayor Cermak of Chicago killed. Zangara electrocuted, March 20, 1933.
Oscar Collazo Griselio Torresola	Harry S. Truman November 1, 1950	Truman not hurt. Guard Coffelt killed, 2 guards injured. Torresola killed at time of attempt. Collazo wounded, death sentence commuted to life imprisonment.
Lee Harvey Oswald	John F. Kennedy November 22, 1963	Kennedy killed. Governor Connally of Texas hurt. Oswald assassinated by Jack Ruby, November 24, 1963.

*Adapted from Weisz and Taylor (1969, p. 660).

ment with the victim, conspiracies for political change, and killings based on personal animosities. The majority of modern assassinations, and particularly those of American presidents, are performed for personal reasons. One man broods for some time over his desire to kill the president, who is often seen as antagonistic to some belief which is cherished by the assassin. The belief may have to do with some personal matter; as a result the president begins to be seen as a personal enemy of the assassin. Evidence in these cases indicates that the assassins were emotionally disturbed.

There appears to be only one exception to the rule that presidential assassins work alone and kill for personal reasons. Oscar Collazo and Griselio Torresola, who attempted to assassinate Truman in 1950, were acting on behalf of the fanatical Puerto Rican Nationalist party, which advocated complete independence for Puerto Rico. At the trial of Collazo (Torresola was killed during the assassination attempt), the prisoner testified that he had hoped that the assassination might lead to a revolution that would enable Puerto Rico to become independent. Attacks on the senate by other members of the party were also carried out.

The assassins

Nine men were involved in the eight assassinations or attempts at assassinations. They were all white males with ages ranging from twenty-four to forty. All were smaller than average in height. With the exception of Lincoln's assassin (Booth), they were unknown people who rose to fame only through their assassination attempt. Five of the nine men were born outside of the United States but all were citizens at the time of the attempt. Only four of the men had married and the marriages of three were disrupted within a short period of time. Seven of the men had shown a deteriorating socioeconomic state in the years preceding the assassination attempts. All used guns, eight of them using handguns and one (Oswald) using a rifle. Each of the men had some grievance against the president that seemed in most cases delusional and obsessional.

In every case but that of Collazo and Torresola there was evidence that the assassin was seriously disturbed. Many had delusions of persecution and grandeur. Lawrence (the unsuccessful assassin of Jackson) believed he was Richard III; Guiteau, Schrank, and Booth each felt that they acted under divine guidance. Czolgolsz had delusions about being poisoned, and Zangara complained of intestinal illness that appears to have been delusional.

Many of the assassins showed excessive ambivalence and distractibility, traits often associated with mental illness. In spite of brooding about their acts for weeks, months, and years, they were often temporarily dissuaded from killing the president. Guiteau and Schrank were armed and in a position to carry out the assassination on several occasions. Guiteau refrained once because Mrs. Garfield was with the president and she looked ill. Zangara intended initially to kill President Hoover, but because he did not want to face the cold weather of Washington, he stayed in Florida and attempted to kill the president-elect instead.

Psychiatrists and psychologists have attempted to make after-the-fact diagnoses of the personality problems of the assassins. A complicating factor is introduced when this is done since an act of homicide would contribute to the likelihood of diagnosing emotional disturbance. However, it is certain that many of the assassins would have been diagnosed as psychologically disturbed even before the killing although the diagnosis might not have been as severe. Hastings (1965) considered six of the assassins to have been paranoid schizophrenics and one other to have had a paranoid personality with psychotic episodes. Freedman (1965) felt that Oswald would have been diagnosed as a sociopathic personality rather than a paranoid schizophrenic.

In addition to considering the psychiatric status of the presidential assassins, workers in this area have tried to understand the personal motivations which led to the killings. Robinson (1965) felt that the assassins did not, on the whole, expect to change the basic political philosophy of the country. Rather, they were seeking immortality and destroying the symbol of the highest authority in the land. The idea that the assassins were seeking immortality is supported by the fact that few of them attempted to conceal their acts. Instead, some sought recognition by boasting of their plans and even letting White House personnel know their intentions.

Again, the need for fame crops up in the fact that three of the assassins made their identity known immediately after the act. Dorpat (1968) saw this as evidence for their need for recognition and possibly also evidence of unconscious suicidal wishes. Dorpat noted that Oswald, who did not confess or advertise himself, left many clues, like fingerprints on his rifle. Perhaps he too wished (albeit unconsciously) for discovery and the attendant notoriety.

The assassins tended to be lonely and alienated from other people. Robinson felt that the animosity of the assassin for the president he killed was not based on actual personal offense, but occurred because the victim symbolized the social order against which the assassin felt a general basic anger. In fact, presidents are much less often threatened with assassination after their terms of office expire; this lends support to the notion that it is the president as a symbol rather than as a person who is attacked.

A presidential assassin

To consider one of these presidential assassins in detail will present a better picture of an assassin, even though the picture may not be typical in all its details. Because it is the most recent, the assassination of Kennedy by Oswald is the most useful to examine. We have more reliable information about Oswald than about any of the other assassins. Although Oswald was killed soon after his arrest, so that we lack information from a postarrest examination, we do have several analyses of Oswald by modern psychologists to draw upon.

In the following description we shall first present some information about his life and life circumstances. Then we shall discuss the conclusions of three analyses of Oswald, analyses based on the theories of personality formulated by Freud, Adler, and Jung respectively.

Lee Harvey Oswald was born in 1939 in New Orleans. His father died of a heart attack two months before Lee's birth, leaving his wife little money to support the baby and his two older brothers. Mrs. Oswald stayed home for Lee's first two years of life but later went to work. When he was three, he was placed in a home for children who had lost one or more parents, joining his brothers who were already there. In 1945 Mrs. Oswald married for the third time and moved to Fort Worth, Texas. Lee went with her while his brothers went to a military academy in Mississippi. In 1948, Mrs. Oswald was divorced from her husband. During the next four years, Lee (aged nine to thirteen) lived alone with his mother in Fort Worth.

The neighbors remember Oswald as being quick to take offense. He was easily provoked to anger and could be quite vicious to other children. His first teacher in elementary school recalled that his mother was rarely at home. His grades deteriorated as he advanced through school, although his IQ tested as 103 at the time.

In 1952, Mrs. Oswald moved to New York to be near one of her other sons. In New York, Lee's behavior was more disturbed. His grades were barely passing. He was judged by his teachers to be uncooperative, undependable, and lacking in self-control. His truancy was so frequent that he was brought before the children's court. The probation officer felt that Mrs. Oswald had no appreciation of her son's psychological problems or her role in them. He advised that Oswald be placed in a psychiatric facility but Mrs. Oswald refused to take him there. The report of a psychiatrist who examined Oswald at this time was reported in *Life*.

> It was apparent that Oswald was an emotionally disturbed, mentally constricted youngster who tended to isolate himself from contacts with others, was suspicious and defiant in his attitude toward authority, and overly sensitive and vengeful

in his relationships with his peers. He saw himself as being singled out for rejection and frustration . . . but did not seem to have developed the courage to act upon his hostility in an aggressive or destructive fashion. He also appeared to be preoccupied about his sexual identity and his future role as a male.

He was guarded, secluded and suspicious in his dealings with the psychiatrist. He had to be reassured that information he gave would not be used against him, but to help him. He could not become verbally productive and talk freely about himself and his feelings. About his mother he would state only that she was "O.K." He had ambivalent feelings about his mother—a strong need for maternal warmth but also an awareness that only a limited amount of affection was available. He protected himself against disappointment by not reaching out to others . . . [He seemed to have] given up hope of making himself understood by anyone about his needs and expectations. In an environment where affection was withheld, he was unable to relate with anyone because he had not learned the techniques and skills which would have permitted it. A diagnosis of incipient schizophrenia was made, based on the boy's detachment from the world and pathological changes in his value systems. His outlook on life had strongly paranoid overtones. The immediate and long-range consequence of these features, in addition to his inability to verbalize hostility, lead to an additional diagnosis:"potential dangerousness." [Jackson, 1964, p. 72]

In 1954, Mrs. Oswald returned with Oswald to New Orleans and Oswald entered eighth grade. His school mates remembered him as a loner, with no friends, and often in fights. In 1955, Oswald entered high school but dropped out within a month. His mother pretended that they had moved away. For the rest of the year, Oswald spent much time reading in the library. He tried to enlist in the Marines when he was sixteen but was rejected because of his age (despite his mother's efforts to help falsify his age). In 1956, Mrs. Oswald and her son moved to Fort Worth and Oswald entered high school there. His school mates described him much as did those in New Orleans but noted that he seemed much more extreme in his behavior than he had four years previously. He soon dropped out again and when he was seventeen joined the Marine Corps. He was described as a loner, unfriendly, and impulsively aggressive. He was sent in 1957 to Japan as a radio technician, where he continued to be isolated and hostile. Although he had a temper, he was not successful in fights. He often used to speak of his name, Lee, and appeared to be proud of it. He felt he had been named after the greatest man in history, Robert E. Lee. (Lee was one of Oswald's father's names.)

He was court-martialed twice in 1958, once for not registering a pistol and once for challenging a noncommissioned officer to fight. He was demoted. In 1958 he was sent to California where he began to learn Russian, his plans for the future apparently decided. He often used to bait officers by challenging them on issues of foreign affairs in order to demonstrate his superior knowledge. He seemed to be in revolt against any authority and was even thrown off the squadron football squad for talking back in the huddle.

In 1959, Mrs. Oswald wrote that she had been injured at work and had no money left, and Oswald was given a hardship discharge. He returned to Fort Worth for three days but soon left by boat for Europe. By mid-October 1959 he was in Russia. He tried to renounce his American citizenship and take Russian citizenship. The Russians refused but allowed him to stay. When interviewed by Western correspondents he seemed pleased by the attention. He was angry with the U. S. Embassy for not letting him renounce his citizenship and protested to the Secretary of the Navy when the Marine Corps gave him a dishonorable discharge for his attempt at renunciation.

The Russians sent Oswald to Minsk and gave him a job in a radio factory for $90 a week. He was soon complaining, about the food, the living quarters, and the political pressures. In 1961, he met a pretty nineteen-year-old pharmacist from Leningrad, whom he married on the rebound from another involvement. Prior to marrying her he had begun negotiations with the U. S. Embassy to return to the United States. He eventually got permission and returned with his wife, Marina, and his newborn daughter. They arrived in Fort Worth in 1962. With some difficulty he got a job as a trainee in a photographic firm and sent for his family. At this time, Marina had left him for a while because he had beaten her for smoking and because she had had her daughter secretly baptized in spite of Oswald's opposition to the ceremony.

In early 1963, Oswald was under a number of pressures. Marina was now pregnant again, and Oswald was fired for incompetence. In March, Oswald bought a gun, giving a false name. On April 10, he disappeared during the evening and came home to claim that he had shot at but missed retired Major General Edwin A. Walker, an advocate of right wing views. Oswald then moved to New Orleans where he obtained an apartment and got a job, but he was soon fired again for incompetence. At this time, he organized a "Fair Play for Cuba" pro-Castro organization of which he was the only member. In September he went to Mexico City to arrange for permission to return to Russia via Cuba, but he was told that it would take three months to process his request. He returned to Dallas where Marina was living, obtained an apartment for himself, and got a job at the Texas Book Depository. At about this time, Marina gave birth to their second child. On November 19, the newspapers announced Kennedy's route through Dallas for his visit on November 22. During his stay in Dallas, Oswald was seen practicing at a local rifle range.

On the evening before Kennedy's visit, Oswald visited Marina, ate dinner, played with his children, and went to bed early. He left early the next morning, without waking anyone, and went to work.

After the assassination, Oswald left the Texas Book Depository and took a bus and then a taxi to his rooming house. He soon left the house, and fifteen minutes later was stopped by Patrolman J. D. Tippet of the Dallas Police. Oswald shot and killed Tippet with a revolver. He entered a nearby cinema but was spotted by the manager of a shoe store who called the police. He was arrested by the police in the cinema after a brief struggle.

During questioning, Oswald denied shooting Kennedy and Tippet. He refused to take a lie detector test. Two days later, while being transferred from the city jail to the county jail, he was approached and shot by Jack Ruby, a nightclub owner.

A psychoanalytic interpretation

No thorough psychoanalytic analysis of Oswald seems to be available, but Katz (1965) speculated about Oswald's motivations and Abrahamsen (1967) discussed certain aspects of the case. (The Adlerian and Jungian analyses which are discussed below were intended to be thorough analyses. Thus, the three interpretations are not really comparable.)

Katz noted that Oswald was the youngest and probably most indulged child of the family. Oswald never knew his father. Lee's mother was estranged from Lee's wife and from her other sons. She loyally defended Lee and appeared to enjoy the publicity she was getting after the assassination. Her defense of Lee was seen by Katz as a defense of herself; that is, an affirmation that she did not err in the way she brought him up.

One might be tempted to say that Kennedy represented Oswald's father, the father who had let him down. But Katz noted that Mrs. Oswald was the overwhelming and domineering figure in her son's life and suggested that the assassination symbolized matricide rather than patricide. Katz saw Oswald's behavior as attempts to shake off his mother — renouncing his country, fleeing to Russia, marrying a Russian. In the end, though, he had to return to the motherland and to mother herself. His panic may have been increased by his becoming a father himself. Katz felt that Oswald's anxiety did not decrease after the assassination and so his behavior (killing Tippet) was aimed at ensuring capture and death by execution.

Why did not Oswald kill his mother then? Katz felt that to do so would be to acknowledge her psychodynamic importance to him (his incestuous desires, or delusions). His denial of the assassination attempt (which is uncommon among presidential assassins) was seen as partly magical wishing (by denying it, he can undo the act) and partly denial of his desires toward his mother. Katz felt that the crucial factor was that Oswald was attempting to be heterosexual and a father but was a failure (or at least limited) here. Had Oswald become asexual or homosexual, Katz felt that he would not have needed to murder the president, since he would have given up the fight against his mother.

Abrahamsen (1967) pointed out a number of factors which support Katz's idea that Oswald's mother was overwhelmingly important in her son's life. Lee's half brother reported that Lee was still sleeping in his mother's bed when he was eleven years old. Other testimony showed that Mrs. Oswald was excessively attached to Lee, that she kept him with her all the time and "spoiled him to death." The one exception to this overintimacy, of course, was the period of time when Lee was about three, when his mother temporarily put him in a Lutheran boarding home. Mrs. Oswald was described by her friends and relatives as a completely self-centered, narcissistic person, who was capable of no compromises. Her closeness to Lee appears to have been based entirely on her own needs. When she could not cope with taking care of Lee, she put him in the boarding home, but she took him out whenever the whim struck her. On Oswald, Abrahamsen commented:

> Keeping Lee close to her all the time may well have exposed him to his mother's intimate sexual experiences and to sexual overstimulation which, during his oedipal stage, would have reinforced his affection and hatred for the intruder, and stirred up considerable castration anxiety and fear in him. His strong ties to his mother, which may have reinforced his "femininity" and undoubted castration fears, showed up later in his pronounced shyness with girls, his attempts to belittle other men, his interest in uniforms and guns, and his loss of sexual interest, ending in impotence, during his marriage. Only for a short time, while in the Marines and in the Union of Soviet Republics, did he exhibit interest in girls, apparently because he was outside his mother's domain. But once he was back in the United States, his need for maternal dependency came through again in his relation both with his mother and with his wife. [P. 873]

Abrahamsen also noted the many misspellings in Oswald's writings, which he considered to be evidence for an immature, exhibitionistic personality, one which would seek fame and recognition through an act which would simultaneously gratify his aggressive needs. (Weinstein and Lyerly [1969] noted that Oswald's misspellings in his letters suggest dyslexia, which sometimes is associated with abnormal electrical activity in the brain and concomitant behavior disturbances, including outbursts of violence. These episodes can be precipitated by emotional stress. This is another possible etiological factor for Oswald's behavior.)

An Adlerian interpretation

Ansbacher, Ansbacher, Shiverick, and Shiverick (1966) noted that an Adlerian analysis of Oswald would show that he had developed a faulty lifestyle because his mother did not develop his trust, friendship, and social interest. A number of points were examined in the Adlerian analysis.

1. *Neglect and inferiority feeling:* It is clear that the absence of a father, the placement of Oswald in a foster home at age two, his mother's remarriage and subsequent divorce led to Oswald's early years being filled with neglect, turmoil, and instability. He did not obtain during these important early formative years the security, regularity, and order that a child needs for healthy development. Oswald reacted to this situation by emphasizing the negative side of existence: the hostility and untrustworthiness of other people.

Every person has some feelings of inferiority. However, a child raised in the situation that Oswald faced will have these feelings in an acute and severe form. Oswald's feelings of inferiority would be exacerbated by his slight stature, his constant shifts of school which would leave him friendless, the absence of a father, and his hearing impairment. These severe feelings of inferiority would lead an individual to be self-centered and to impair his social interest and this is apparent in the "loner" style developed by Oswald. When friends gave him gifts on the birth of his baby, he could not accept them and felt that his friends' motives were humiliating charity.

2. *Pampered lifestyle:* Adler suggested that three factors can lead a child to have poor opinions of himself and the world and to develop a neurotic, self-centered lifestyle: being neglected or unwanted, being pampered, and having organ inferiority. Mrs. Oswald seems to have both neglected Oswald in some respects and pampered him in others. The neglect has been touched on above. The pampering is shown by the way in which she let him have his own way and excused him of responsibility for his actions.

She condoned his truancy. She protected him from the law and from psychiatrists and placed the blame for his actions on others. Oswald developed, as expected therefore, a belief that he was entitled to special privileges and not bound to rules that others must follow. Organ inferiority was present in his hearing impairment and his short stature.

3. *Marxism:* Oswald was not able to see that his lack of satisfaction stemmed from his own failure to contribute. He concluded that his lack must be the fault of others and the society that was exploiting him. Thus, the philosophy espoused by Marx appealed to him. He saw happiness and utopia through Marxism and so began his interest in Russia which was capped by his decision to live in Russia and become a citizen.

4. *Grandiosity:* Oswald wanted to be superior to everyone else. To this end, he challenged those above him, resulting in his being court-martialed in the Marine Corps and being thrown off the football squad. He also set himself unrealistic goals. He enrolled in a small institution for higher learning in Switzerland (but never went). He planned to write a book about Russia on his return to the United States (but never did). In Russia he

was pleased to cast himself as a defector and pose for photographs and be interviewed.

However, such a goal is bound to come into conflict with reality. Oswald was too ordinary to succeed in being important. He was denied citizenship in Russia, he failed in social relationships, in his work, and in his marriage. His rigid and hostile manner alienated potential friends. He worked at unskilled jobs and was often fired for incompetence. His wife berated him for his failure to earn enough to support the family and for his sexual inadequacies. He offered to work for an anti-Castro Cuban group but was rejected; he then distributed pro-Castro Cuban leaflets and was fined for disturbing the peace. He was denied an easy return to Russia.

One way he sought to restore and maintain his self-esteem was through guns. He was a good marksman, and in 1963 he had his wife photograph him holding in one hand a Trotskyite newspaper and in the other a rifle—a true revolutionary. The assassination was the result of a coincidence. The chance occurrence that led Kennedy's route past the place where he worked gave Oswald the opportunity to act in a way that resolved many of his problems: the act would make him famous, express his hostility toward superiors and his own country, and would enable him to use his cherished rifle with which he was so skillful. It is most unlikely that the assassination was part of a long-term plan. (Again, Oswald differs in this from most of the other presidential assassins.)

A Jungian interpretation

Progoff (1967) noted the absence of a father figure as an important fact in Oswald's life. His natural father died before he was born, his stepfather was around for only four years, and he was in an institution for a time. Progoff felt that this meant for Oswald that there was a gap in his experience of his own origins. One's father serves as a connection with past generations, a link with history. These transpersonal aspects of the father set the basis for the young man's first feelings of his own identity and of his own value. It helps start the growth process. Oswald lacked this initial assistance in developing to the point at which the individual can legitimately overthrow the assumed identity and achieve a new personal identity.

The mother plays a large role for the fatherless child, who will come to absorb her traits (consciously and unconsciously) and develop a derivative lifestyle. The young man enacts the ideas and values of his mother as if they were his own. Should the mother possess unhealthy traits, the man will suffer. Mrs. Oswald, who was often under economic pressure, developed into a hard woman with a false sense of masculinity with which to shield herself from society. She was a hard worker and rigid organizer. She was opinionated and externalized the blame for misfortunes. Progoff felt that Oswald endured many hardships as a consequence of being the child of this erratic widow.

In adolescence, the person must reject his childlike life and destroy it, for only then can he begin to build a life that is truly his own. Oswald was impeded in this in many respects: the emotional poverty of his childhood, his feelings of inferiority which he had dealt with by fanciful wishes of being famous and powerful, and the excessive neurotic isolation of his early teenage years. For Oswald, this period was one of greater psychological turbulence than is usual.

Oswald obtained some relief from the tension of this period in his study of Marxism. In this, it was as if he tried to compensate for the meagerness of his personal existence by embracing a utopian view of the world. His emigration to Russia was a symbolic rejection of his old environmental values in order to begin to construct a more satisfying belief structure. However, he was unsuccessful here for Russia refused him citizenship.

Progoff saw Oswald's marriage as an aspect of his search for meaning. Oswald thought he was marrying a dedicated communist, but he soon must have realized that she was normal in her love of material things. Oswald saw in Marina the embodiment of a new set of values which he had not yet been able to make real in his own life. But when his projection was checked against the reality of the wife, she was found not to be the dedicated utopian he had envisioned. His marital problems, which included his wife's leaving him and refusing to return, meant that all the paths he had tried to develop a new identity were closed to him. (On the night before the assassination, Marina refused Oswald's offer to buy her a washing machine. She was living with a friend and did not intend to return to him. Her rejection may have symbolized the other frustrating rejections he had received in his life.)

Progoff noted that the frustration attendant upon blocks in a person's attempts to be reborn, to become a new person, is quite different from blocks in his attempts to achieve some material goal. It is a stoppage of the life process itself. At such a point, the possibilities of psychological growth have come to a dead end. Only an act of great destructive force can serve to release so fundamental a frustration. If this violence is turned outward, the object destroyed must be some symbolic representation of the old self. Ever since he had read Marx, America, his mother country, had been the symbol of his old self to Oswald. By chance, he was able to destroy the one man who symbolically represented this country.

Conclusions

We have presented the ways in which three personality theories have viewed and analyzed the motivations behind an assassin's actions. More appropriate than trying to judge which is best is an attempt to assimilate their contributions in order to come to an understanding of Oswald. In any psychological explanation, there often remains a gap, a feeling "but why should one man in many million act so?" Progoff's views on this conclude this chapter.

That these two chains of events [Oswald's and Kennedy's lives] which had no causal relationship to each other should meet so conveniently may well be considered to be chance. But the impulse to action at the given moment was more than chance. Nonetheless, it cannot be understood merely as an act of arbitrary personal decision; nor can it be understood as an event that was psychologically determined. Some additional factor was present, and it was this factor that crystallized the situation, giving shape and form to its component events.

What is this formative factor? It is mercurial, too intangible to be analytically described; but it is real and its effects are visible. A myth is not only an outwardly false belief about something. It may also be the quintessence of truth, at once the core and the context of meaning, providing both the formative factor that crystallizes a situation and also its significance, its meaning in the larger continuity of life. . . .

It is as if they [Oswald and Kennedy] were both caught up and victimized by a transpersonal patterning of events, an active principle which uncannily crossed the boundaries of time and causality, and brought a mythic event into the actuality of history. [Pp. 46-47]

Chapter 8

Threats
of murder

Although murder is relatively common in the United States, threats of murder are frequent and probably far exceed the actual number of killings. It is interesting that murder threats, unlike suicide threats, are generally taken rather seriously (with some exceptions which will be discussed below). The folk psychology which declares about suicide that "those who talk about it won't do it" is rarely applied to murder. Perhaps this is because the threatened person is understandably anxious to save his own skin and so pays attention to threats even when he thinks the event is rather unlikely. Another reason might be that suicide is an idea surrounded with a good deal more anxiety than the thought of murder. Suicide is a taboo topic, while murder is a subject upon which mystery novels are based.

Threatening murder

One investigation (Macdonald, 1963) looked at 100 psychiatric patients who had been hospitalized specifically because they threatened to kill someone. The threateners varied considerably in the specifics of the behavior which had brought about their admission to the hospital. Some had made the threat directly to the victim, while others had told other people that there was someone they intended to kill. Some had made only one threat, while others repeated their threats over a number of years. Sometimes the threats appeared serious to the listener; in other cases they seemed to be jokes.

The apparent joking nature of some murder threats does not minimize their potential seriousness. In one case, a soldier calmly informed a fellow soldier that he was going to kill a certain noncommissioned officer. The next day he shot the NCO and returned to his barracks to announce his act with the words "Mission accomplished, mind at ease." He then asked one soldier to notify the commanding officer and requested that another play the tune "In the jailhouse now."

In the group that Macdonald studied, the patients tended to have problems with the expression of hostility. Some tended to be aggressive in an impulsive way when anyone criticized or annoyed them. Others had been involved in sadistic behavior throughout their lives and boasted about their sadistic exploits. Several of the patients expressed their hostility less directly by keeping large private armories or vicious dogs. There were also some patients who were generally not at all aggressive; they rarely got angry and in fact seemed to have trouble in expressing any aggressiveness at all (See chapter 15).

About 35 percent of the patients either had childhood experiences of parental brutality or had experienced direct or indirect attempts at seduction by their parents. The experience of parental brutality could predispose the person to later aggressiveness by hurting and frustrating him so that he felt an unusual amount of hostility, or he could simply learn that adults should behave aggressively. In the case of parental seduction, pain and fear might create hostility. A family which did not conform to social strictures in one area might be less likely to do so in other areas and so would not teach the child the usual social disapproval of excessive aggressiveness. Furthermore, the family in which the parents have little control over their sexual impulses is probably one in which the children are not taught general impulse control.

About one-half of the patients were judged to be psychotic. Most of them were diagnosed as suffering from schizophrenia or from organic brain disease. Among the nonpsychotic patients, the most common diagnosis was the character disorder passive-aggressive personality.

To a rather large extent, the murder threats made by Macdonald's patients were a family matter. About 80 percent of the threats were made to relatives, with the majority directed toward spouses. Some 37 percent of the patients contemplated or threatened suicide at the time of the murder threat. (The following of an actual murder by suicide is much more common when the person killed is a close relative.) But these statistics do not give a complete picture of the family patterns involved in the murder threat. The threat was generally part of a consistent pattern of family relationships in which both the threatener and the threatened were active. Many of the recipients of threats helped bring on the threat by provoking the patient in some way (See chapter 2 on victim-precipitated homicide). The threatened people, although they were distressed by the threat, were often highly reluctant to seek help, protection, or advice. The murder threat was seemingly a reflection of some important interpersonal process and had come about because both the threatener and the threatened needed it. In spite of their trepidation, the threatened people continued the relationship, much as a battered child desires nothing better than to be reunited with the parents who beat him (Scott, 1962).

For example,

> a 35 year-old alcoholic often threatened to kill his wife and frequently beat her and the children. After one such threat and a severe beating he put her in his car and drove around with the stated intention of looking for a mine shaft in which to bury her. Once while he was beating one of his children, his wife went to load a shotgun, but he took the gun away from her and clubbed her with the butt. She would turn white, according to a neighbour, when she heard her husband's car in the driveway and the children would fearfully scurry around the house picking up their toys and putting things straight in the living room. One child had mild deafness from blows on the head. The wife made no effort to seek help and when her mother notified the court, she opposed the efforts of the court to protect the children from further mistreatment. [Macdonald, 1963, p. 128]

Do people who threaten murder usually carry out their threats? Not all of them do, of course, but the proportion of eventual killings among people who have threatened murder is a good deal higher than among those who never mention the subject. In Macdonald's group (Macdonald, 1967), three murdered someone and four killed themselves in the five years after the study. This proportion is rather high, especially considering that, when one looks at actual murderers paroled from prison, within twenty years only one in 200 has killed again.

Threatening to kill the president

Disturbed people are commonly preoccupied with the president and regard him either as the source of all their troubles or as the person who could right their wrongs. Milton Rokeach (1964), in *The Three Christs of Ypsilanti*, quotes a letter from a psychiatric patient to President Kennedy, requesting that he be brought to Washington and given a job in the government. In these cases, the president is not being thought of as the individual person he really happens to be, but instead as a symbol of power and authority. An emotionally disturbed person may feel that if he could intimidate or kill the symbolic person, he could coerce the power of the government into doing whatever he wants.

Preoccupation with the president as the source of power, and threats or attempts to kill him, have been in existence as long as the country. Most people became aware of the frequency and seriousness of these problems after the wave of assassinations which began with President Kennedy's death. Because the president's life is guarded so carefully, the number of actual or attempted assassinations is far smaller than the number of assassination threats. According to Weinstein and Lyerly (1969), the number of men who were arrested or hospitalized for assassination threats between 1945 and 1965 amounted to 137—about six every year. In addition to these, of course, there were others who made their threats in such a form that they were not apprehended.

Actually, most of the threatening letters received by the president include a good deal of personal information and are signed, making it easy to catch the threatener. The letters give the impression that the threatener is trying to establish some emotional relationship with the president and is also using the letter to establish a personal identity. The threateners had no plan for escape from the consequence of their letters. This self-destructive tendency was also evident in the overt and covert threats of suicide contained in the letters.

Weinstein and Lyerly obtained some social data on the 137 threateners. Their average age was thirty-six years, with a range of fourteen to seventy-six. Socially speaking, they tended to be isolated. Thirty-eight percent came from broken homes and only 26 percent were married. Another 22 percent were divorced or separated. Only 26 percent were employed at the time of the threat. The most frequent social association had been with the armed forces; 60 percent had been in the service; 8 percent of these had been discharged dishonorably. Sixty percent of the threateners had previously been hospitalized for psychiatric problems, and 23 percent had histories of alcoholism or drug addiction.

All of the assassination threats occurred when the person was in a situation of general stress. In about 10 percent of the cases, it was possible to find some precipitating event such as being fired from a job or being in a fight or argument, but in most cases no particular stressful event could be noted. In some cases, the assassination threat seemed to have the function of making sure that the offender was not released from an institution at which he felt safe, or ensuring that he was quickly put in such an institution.

The following is a typical case of an assassination threat against the president.

> This young man who was admitted . . . in October of 1963 had written the following letter to President Kennedy the previous May: "Dear President Kenny. The reason I wrote this letter I am going to kill you. Don't me lie but there is one reason I don't like to do this. Forgive me but you have to die." [signed with name and address]
>
> During the previous February he had broken up with a woman friend, subsequently becoming quite depressed, with suicidal ideation. He began to be convinced that the only way to handle the situation would be to rejoin the military service, from which he had been discharged 13 years previously, after an apparent suicide gesture. He had already tried unsuccessfully to re-enter the service many times. Finally, he decided that, if he wrote a letter threatening the President, this would get some action. He later indicated that some of the anger in the letter was really directed at the woman friend, to whom he had written a threatening letter three days prior to the Presidential threat. He also indicated that he had been willing to accept death as a punishment.

The patient had been born and raised in a rural Appalachian region, in a family of limited resources, 1 of 15 siblings. At age 17 he had joined the service, but after his suicide gesture, he was given a general discharge under honorable conditions. Significantly, he tended to consider it a dishonorable discharge. He had always been uncomfortable with women and had an unsuccessful marriage, ending in divorce when the wife left him.

The patient [was] presented as a rather naive, uneducated, simple appearing young man, but conveyed a certain warmth in his manner. He communicated an exceptionally strong feeling of guilt. Clinical findings were consistent with a diagnosis of schizophrenic reaction, simple type, with depressive features.

At the time of the assassination, the patient appeared depressed and said he was getting the feeling of being the actual murderer himself. He later said that if he had known such a thing would actually happen, he would never have written the letter. He said he felt particularly sorry for "her" (Mrs. Kennedy), and that, "seeing her standing there by the coffin, with the children," had brought home the full significance of the event. He also indicated that he almost felt as if the actual fact of his being in prison at the time was the only concrete evidence that he was not the assassin himself. [Rothstein, 1964, p. 246]

Rothstein (1964) examined eight cases of threatened assassinations and felt that the people he talked to bore a considerable resemblance to Lee Harvey Oswald (see chapter 7). All Rothstein's cases were diagnosed as schizophrenic. Their mothers, like Oswald's, had in many cases been unable to meet their sons' emotional needs. The fathers were often not prominent in the boys' lives, being dead, absent, or ineffective. Two-thirds of the cases had been in the military services. Almost all of them had a history of depression and suicidal tendencies. The assassination threats seemed to be a way to seek punishment and help at the same time.

Rothstein felt that the typical case of threatened assassination takes the following course. The child is deprived of maternal care because the mother is absent or simply lacks the emotional capacity to care for her children properly. The lack of maternal contact leads to a severe rage against women. This anger, in turn, makes it difficult for the man to form a mature heterosexual relationship as an adult. In addition, the man cannot get along with males in authority because of his excessive anger and rebellious nature. He turns his anger overtly toward men rather than women, although his basic rage is against women, because it was safer for him to be angry at his absent father than at his mother, who at least fulfilled some of his needs.

In adolescence, the man becomes aware of the unsatisfactory nature of his family and turns at an early age toward a larger organization, usually the military. Military service provides him with many emotional benefits. It satisfies his dependency needs and allows him to identify with a meaningful group. It provides masculine figures to identify with, thus filling an unsatisfied need. It provides the controls over his behavior which he has never learned to employ by himself. It also removes him from women, an important source of frustration and annoyance. But, although the military service serves all these functions for the man, it cannot fulfill his unrealistic hopes for achievement and belonging, and he begins to see it as a new frustration.

The frustrated man then turns against the military and against the government as a whole. He turns to political groups which are opposed to the United States. The rage which was previously displaced from the mother to male authority figures is thus displaced once more, to the government of the United States. It is eventually focused upon the president as the embodiment of governmental power. From this point of view, a threat to assassinate the president is at one level an expression of anger against the threatener's own father, but at a deeper level an expression of anger against his mother.

Chapter 9

Murder as an institution

In the great majority of cultures, the commandment "Thou shalt not kill" has been rewritten "Thou shalt kill, but thou shalt do so only under culturally prescribed circumstances." The book of Leviticus delineates the conditions under which the ancient Jews were specifically directed to punish certain actions by carrying out the act prohibited by the Tables of the Law. Institutionalized killing has been used in various cultures for purposes of punishment and, law enforcement, as a means of population control, as a religious rite, and as a form of entertainment for the populace. Cultures which carry on wars, of course, not only sanction but encourage and reward murder of specified persons at specified times.

Murder as population control

Infanticide has been a common means of population control in some cultures. Tahitian women at the time of the cruise of the *Bounty* strangled or drowned unwanted infants. The Australian aborigines used infanticide to insure that no new child need be cared for until the next youngest was three or four years of age. The legend of Oedipus reveals how unwanted babies in ancient Greece were left to die of exposure or be killed by animals. Roman fathers had the power to decide whether any of their newborn children were to live or die. These old customs gradually came into disapproval in Europe, although infanticide long continued to be a common way for an illegitimately pregnant girl to save herself from disgrace. Mary Hamilton, the heroine of the Scottish folk song, having "borne a babe to the highest Stuart of all," tried to escape the consequences by placing the child in a "wee boat" and floating it out to sea.

Less commonly, control of population is carried out by the murder of old people who can no longer contribute enough to justify their consumption of food. This occurs among the Eskimo and other groups under severe environmental pressure.

Murder as a religious rite

The sacrifice of human lives for religious purposes has generally involved victims who were in no position to argue. The Mayas sacrificed prisoners of war, the Druids burned alive in wicker baskets victims who were chosen by lot, and the Carthaginians and others sacrificed infants and young children. The magical significance of killing children lingered in European thought well into the Christian era. Witches were believed to murder and even cannibalize infants in order to gain satanic knowledge and power (Despert, 1965). The weird sisters in *Macbeth* used a "finger of birth strangled babe" to concoct a potion. During periods of anti-Semitic feeling, medieval Jews were commonly charged with the kidnap and murder of a Christian child in connection with the "magical" rites of the Passover celebration.

The death penalty

Punishment by death for certain crimes has not been universal, but societies which have not used it are much rarer than those which have. The Mosaic code listed three dozen capital offenses. The number of crimes punishable by death has varied considerably in English common law and in the United States. At the end of the fifteenth century, English law provided that treason, murder of a husband by his wife, malicious murder, larceny, robbery, burglary, rape, and arson be punished by death. The number of capital crimes later increased, so that it has been estimated that 223 offenses could be punished by execution in the early nineteenth century. In the American colonies, the capital statutes varied from place to place (as they do today) and from time to time. The Massachusetts Bay Colony in 1636 had thirteen capital crimes, while Virginia laws of the early nineteenth century provided the death penalty for seventy offenses by blacks and five offenses in the case of whites (Bedau, 1967).

Murder as entertainment

The risking of life in order to entertain an audience has been and is common in the form of bullfights, automobile races, and so on. Some societies, like that of

ancient Rome, have developed highly ritualized pro-
ductions in which conflicts between men, or between
men and wild beasts, have led to the almost certain
death of some of the participants. In more recent times,
too, public executions have been provided for the
delectation of the populace. Thackeray described the
excitement of the crowds watching a public execution
in 1840:

> I must confess . . . that the sight has left on my
> mind an extraordinary feeling of terror and shame.
> It seems to me that I have been abetting an act of
> frightful wickedness and violence, performed by a
> set of men against one of their fellows; and I pray
> God that it may soon be out of the power of any
> man in England to witness such a hideous and
> degrading sight. Forty thousand persons (say the
> Sheriffs), of all ranks and degrees—mechanics,
> gentlemen, pickpockets, members of both Houses
> of Parliament, street-walkers, newspaper-writers,
> gather together before Newgate at a very early
> hour: the most part of them give up their natural
> quiet night's rest, in order to partake of this
> hideous debauchery, which is more exciting than
> sleep, or than wine, or the last new ballet, or any
> other amusement they can have. [quoted by
> Bedau, 1967, pp. 2-3]

Although executions in recent years were performed in private in the United States, the occurrence
of an execution may call forth emotions not unlike
those of people in past times. One of the present
authors recalls the scene in a dormitory of a well-known

New England women's college at the hour when Caryl Chessman was scheduled to die: a young woman gigglingly played the *Dead March* on the piano while a countdown was carried out.

Genocide as a behavior pattern

Particular cultural patterns and combinations of attitudes and beliefs can lead to institutionalized mass murder in the form of genocide—a deliberate, systematic attempt to exterminate a racial, political, or cultural group. Throughout the history of man, genocide has been the rule rather than the exception. Whenever powerful forces have invaded new territories, they have tried to exterminate the indigenes or reduce them to servitude. Invaders destroy the symbols treasured by their victims (temples, sanctuaries, shrines, and so on), pillage homes, rape the women, and carry off the defeated into slavery or leave them as servants of the conquerors. If the invaded people are strong in force of arms or have a long-established culture, the two peoples may eventually become allies, not only through the maintenance of successful armed resistance, but by the quiet integration of the two sets of values and of social and political institutions. The extremes range from the extermination of the conquered (as in some Biblical wars) to the assimilation of the conquerors (as in the eventual results of the Norman Conquest).

The Renaissance and Reformation led to a change in attitudes toward genocide. Previously, genocide was seen as acceptable behavior, for the society was deemed more important than the individual. After the Renaissance, however, respect for human personality grew, and the individual emerged as the basic unit in human relations. Further, as religious and political power were gradually separated, genocide lost one of its most powerful sources of energy—the fanatical drive to religious proselytization.

However, genocide continued to thrive in the colonial efforts of European nations. The Spanish invaders destroyed the pre-Colombian cultures of the Americas, in particular the Aztecs and the Incas. The Indians of North America were slowly decimated, and even today some South American nations are systematically exterminating the Indians of their continent. Many of these genocidal acts did not lead to complete extermination, but because of their severity there is much evidence of guilt in the attitudes of the governments of the United States and Australia toward their indigenous peoples.

After the American Revolution of 1776 and the French Revolution of 1789, genocide was no longer admissible in the best European thinking, either theoretically or morally. The Declaration of the Rights of Man and the Declaration of Independence led toward the full emancipation of man and modern democracy. However, the only guarantee against genocide continued to be a voluntary adherence to principles since there was (and is) no real force to hold genocidal acts in check. Not all human beings were included within the early democratic attitudes, as is exemplified by the Declaration of Independence for white males simultaneously with the maintenance of slavery and attempts to exterminate the American Indians.

Genocide has not usually been specifically condemned by law. However, at the Hague Convention in 1907, during which international laws were formulated, the rules included guidelines that condemned genocide.

The convention stated that the military authority in an occupied country must respect the honor and rights of the families and the lives of the individuals under their control. Sanctions for contravention of these rules were never specified. This absence of of precisely defined codes, legal sanctions, and soundly established procedures for judgment of war crimes resulted in much judicial argument after World War II.

Cormier (1966) made a moral distinction between genocide committed by developed and by underdeveloped nations. Genocides committed by free modern nations who have temporarily lost their sense of liberty and justice he called *regressive genocides*; these, he felt, are pathological and should be halted by outside forces. However, since genocide has been part of the history of all nations, and since genocide was common in our heritage in periods of rapid social evolution, one cannot expect developing nations to evolve without passing through similar periods. Undesirable though genocide may be under any circumstances, Cormier felt, genocide in nations developing today should be seen not as pathological but as a normal phase of development.

The most recent genocides have produced little involvement among the nations of the world. The Hindu-Muslim wars in Asia and the Nigerian civil war seem safely distant, even though constant newspaper reports have been available. In the case of the extermination of Indians in Brazil, involvement is slight because few people have even read about the problem. The last genocidal actions that did manage to arouse worldwide indignation were those of the Germans in their attempts to exterminate the Jews some thirty years ago. We describe this in some detail in order to throw light on the problem of genocide.

The genocide of the Jews

The history of anti-Semitism began long before the advent of Christianity. Communities of Jews in pre-Christian empires were sometimes tolerated but often persecuted. Although as citizens of their countries they participated in the local economic and political activities, their religion often held them apart from their neighbors. Cormier has implied that if there had not been a religiously fanatical, proselytizing group among the Jews of these countries, then anti-Semitism might well not have existed. Though this may be disputed, it is obvious that as long as a group remains unassimilated, the potential for scapegoating exists.

After the advent of Christianity, anti-Semitism continued, fueled by the ecclesiastical and theological conflicts of the early church. The early Christians even tried to justify their anti-Semitism on the grounds that the Jews were guilty of deicide. The corollary was to interpret the dispersion of the Jews as their punishment for having fallen from grace. If they survived in shame, they would bear witness to their guilt. As Cormier put it:

> The witnesses must be humiliated, but their victimization must never lead to their total annihilation; their existence is necessary as evidence. The history of the Jews in our civilization seems like a clever game of cat-and-mouse. [P. 283]

Although the Jews during the first 1,000 years of Christianity were excluded from public office, forced to convert, and persecuted in other ways, there was not yet genocide—deportations, the wearing of distinctive emblems, extermination. This became increasingly likely in the last 1,000 years.

By the tenth and eleventh centuries, there was a history of anti-Semitism such that it could become a popular prejudice with a long tradition. Eventually the prejudice grew until the roles of persecutors and victims were clearly defined.

The persecution and genocide of the Jews developed rapidly during the Crusades. At times anti-Semitism was dealt with harshly by the authorities, but at other times the same governments would encourage and exploit it. Anti-Semitism became an outlet for the psychopathology of modern man, a way of resolving conscious and unconscious conflicts and anxieties.

Anti-Semitism completed its growth into genocide in twentieth-century Germany, with serious attempts not only to scapegoat but to exterminate the Jews. With the exceptions of a few famous men who were allowed to live for the sake of appearances, the Germans in the 1930s and 1940s tried to kill everyone of Jewish ancestry in the lands they occupied. The total killed in the extermination camps is estimated to be about six million people.

Several features of this genocidal period are of psychological interest.

1. *Denial.* The horrors described during the war were often felt by distant nations to be exaggerated war propaganda. Nations continued to ignore the evidence and make pacts with Germany, blinding themselves to the realities. Denial was no longer possible after the war when the existence of the extermination camps was seen and recorded on film.

2. *Resignation to persecution.* Thousands of years ago the Jews gave up attempts to found a Judaic kingdom and focused on the spiritual and social message of Judaism divorced from political aspirations. This attitude has appeared to non-Jews as resignation, but it was not inertia, emotional paralysis, or masochistic acceptance of suffering. It was rather a passive resistance, a refusal to respond actively to physical or political attack.

However, resignation became for many Jews a neurotic solution, and thus exceeded the attitude taught by Jewish tradition. Not all Jews were so resigned, of course. Especially among the Zionists, the opposite qualities were to the fore. But among those remaining in Germany and neighboring areas, the resignation of the Jews was sometimes pathological, a sad legacy of a thousand years of sick anti-Semitism. As Bettelheim (1960) has said of the Jews under the Nazi regime:

> All of them were the vanguard of a walk toward the peace of death . . . that the SS then killed them is of less importance than the fact that they marched themselves into death, choosing to give up a life that was no longer human. [P. 299]

3. *The persecutors.* In recent decades, much research has been conducted on prejudice, enabling some understanding of the narrow perspective and social attitudes of prejudiced individuals. In his authoritarianism, the prejudiced person is often simultaneously subservient to those in power over him and brutal to those below him. The majority of Germans of the Nazi era, living under the despotism of sadistic, deranged

leaders, may have feared to act and prepared instead to live in passive guilt. But it may also be the case that virulent anti-Semitism satisfied pathological needs in them, needs that have also fueled lesser forms of prejudice.

Cormier has noted that genocide is not past. There will be genocides in the future, genocides that may be unpreventable because the armed force required to stop them would in itself be genocidal. For the problem of genocide, there are no answers, only uncertainties. As Cormier has said, "There are crimes which make men afraid, there are crimes which make us afraid of being men . . . (Cormier, 1966, p. 276)."

Studying institutionalization

The extent to which murder is institutionalized in a culture is reflected in the attitudes toward violence held by individuals within the culture. Some studies on the understanding of attitudes toward violence have recently been carried out by Blumenthal (1972). She felt that the level of violence within a culture is determined by the interaction of opposing forces, which may act to eliminate violent actions or make extreme violence a justifiable activity. Five forces were considered to be acting in the Western world:

1. Basic cultural values against violence, like those of the Ten Commandments and the Golden Rule.

2. Basic cultural values in favor of violence, like the glorification of outlaws and gangsters.

3. Identification with the person or group carrying out an aggressive act. (This may be positive, in which case the act is likely to be seen as justifiable, or negative, in which case the violent action will be condemned.)

4. Identification with victims of aggression may also be positive, leading to disapproval of the violent act, or negative, resulting in the belief that the act is justifiable.

5. Definitions of violent behavior may vary, and an action which is destructive or forceful but not defined as violent may not require justification in terms of other cultural attitudes. This is especially notable in Blumenthal's study since 58 percent of the American men tested considered that burning a draft card is violence *in and of itself* (not only in its capacity as a cause of violence); 38 percent said that student protest is violence; and 22 percent felt that sit-ins are violence. Only 35 percent defined "police shooting looters" as violence, and only 56 percent considered "police beating students" to be violence. Blumenthal concluded from her study:

> that attitudes toward violence are strongly related to basic values, attitudes toward others, and the language used to describe events. The fact that the levels of violence considered to be justified can be predicted (at least in the statistical sense) from a model based on values and beliefs about others implies that violence is not an aberrant or asocial phenomenon, but an integral part of the culture in which we live. If such is the case, positive attitudes toward violence will not be changed before reorientations in other areas of American life take place. [P. 1302]

These statements are undoubtedly true of the institutionalization of murder in most cultures, times, and places.

Chapter 10

Murder in other cultures

Information about the United States alone makes it clear that the tendency to murder, and the circumstances in which murder is committed, vary widely because of cultural differences. The reader would be correct if he predicted a wide variation in homicidal behavior from country to country, as well as from subculture to subculture. First of all, there is a considerable range over which homicide rates vary for different countries. Wolfgang (1967) determined rates for some representative countries around 1960. (See table 8 for our version of his information. Of course, we have no way of knowing the accuracy of these figures since the compilation of statistics varies drastically from country to country; but they are suggestive of the extent to which humans vary in their tendency to murder.)

TABLE 8

Variations in homicide rates*

Country	Rate per 100,000 per year
Colombia	34.0
Mexico	31.1
South Africa	21.2
Burma	10.8
Turkey	6.1
Chile	4.9
Uruguay	4.6
United States	4.5
Nigeria	4.4
Ceylon	4.3
Finland	2.9
Bulgaria	2.7
United Arab Republic	2.3
Peru	2.3
Poland	2.1
Japan	1.9
France	1.7
Hungary	1.6
Australia	1.5
Canada	1.4
Italy	1.4
Jordan	1.2
Hong Kong	1.0
Switzerland	0.9
Spain	0.8
Belgium	0.7
Sweden	0.7
England/Wales	0.6
Iceland	0.6
Denmark	0.5
Norway	0.5
Netherlands	0.3
Eire	0.2

*Adapted from Wolfgang (1967)

To go into the reasons for these cultural variations in murder rate would require a book on the economic conditions and child-rearing practices of each country.

It may be more fruitful, in our limited space, to discuss some special ways in which homicide occurs in particular cultures. A number of societies have particularly interesting forms of homicide which differ from the murders found in most of Western society. We will discuss three such forms: the amok syndrome of Malaya, the Wiitiko psychosis of the Canadian Cree and Ojibwa, and the political murders of Acan in Mexico.

The Amok Syndrome

Running amok is no mere figure of speech, but a real homicidal syndrome. The behavior can best be illustrated through a case reported by an eyewitness (Burton-Bradley, 1968).

The subject approached some of his relatives and the witness at dusk one evening while they were sitting outside a house. The subject had a spear, which he threw at one of the relatives, who was hit in the side. The victim was carried inside the house by some of the others. While this was being done, the subject threw another spear which hit another relative, who removed it herself. Everyone ran away, defending himself in the process. The eyewitness reported that the subject said, "Where are you all? I am coming after you." The witness hid until daybreak. He then found two bodies, one inside the house and one outside. With five other villagers, he searched for the subject and found him in the bush, wounded in the chest, with five spears stuck in the ground beside him. He was overpowered. In addition to having attacked and killed people, he had damaged and destroyed yams in the yam house.

When arrested, the subject said that he had been in the bush for two days without food, prior to the offense. He claimed to have amnesia for his acts but admitted that it was said that he had killed a man and a woman and speared three others. However, he later admitted that at the time of the offense he was aware that his actions were wrong in the eyes of his own people and of the administration, and that they might lead to his death. After he was admitted to a psychiatric hospital, no mental disorder was noted.

Amok is a behavior characterized by previous brooding, homicidal outbursts, persistence in reckless homicide without apparent motive, and a claim of amnesia. It is best known as a behavior of the Malays. Various authors have seen its cause in malaria, pneumonia, cerebral syphilis, hashish, heat stroke, paranoid states, and mania. However, Wulfften-Palthe (1933) suggested that amok was a standardized form of emotional release. The community recognizes it as such and expects it of an individual placed in an intolerably embarrassing or shameful situation. Malaysian social structure stresses strong kinship ties, which lead to tensions arising from interpersonal obligations. Wulfften-Palthe noted that amok was rare (if not absent) in Malays living in Europe (that is, without immediate kinship obligations), and among subjects removed from their social group. Ewing (1955) has observed that a Moro of the Philippines often asks his parents for permission before running amok.

Burton-Bradley (1968) summarized his experiences of amok cases, all of whom were young men who exhibited no symptoms of epilepsy, schizophrenia, or any other kind of mental disorder.

A healthy young adult is quieter than usual or "goes bush" for a few days. There may be a history of slight or insult. He may regain his normal composure, or the condition may continue and remain unchanged (an abortive attack), or it may become worse. In this case, suddenly and without warning, without anyone expecting such an immediate response at this point of time, he jumps up, seizes an axe or some spears, rushes around attacking all and sundry and even destroying inanimate objects, such as yam houses or hospital property. Within a very short period of time, a number of people will be dead or wounded. He shouts "I am going to kill you," and everyone in the neighborhood seeks safety in flight. All are now fully aware that the man is suffering from a special form of "kava kava" or "long long" (insanity), that he will not be satiated or stop of his own accord. They recognize that this, and similar types of reaction, are available methods of tension reduction, used from time to time as acts arising from despair. The man continues in this fashion until overpowered, by which time he has become exhausted. He may also be killed or wounded. The attack may be aborted at any time by anyone who is brave enough to attempt it. On the subject's recovery, it is usually claimed that there is no recollection of the events that occurred during the acute phase. [P. 252]

Burton-Bradley felt that the killings were envisaged as a means of delivering the subject from unbearable situations. Much thinking precedes the nihilistic feeling of despair. The man sees his life as intolerable and has nothing to lose but life, so he trades his own for those of others. The amok rehabilitates him in the eyes of his group, but he runs the risk of being killed in the process. However, Burton-Bradley felt that in true cases of amok, the man is not making a rational decision; he does completely lose control and his strong emotions take over.

The syndrome is most commonly found in Malaya, but has been reported in Trinidad, India, Liberia, Siberia, Africa, and Polynesia. The behavior is best conceptualized as caused by individual idiosyncracies in personality, psychological precipitating factors, and group expectations.

The Wiitiko Psychosis

According to Parker (1960), Wiitiko psychosis is a behavior pattern reported for the Cree and Ojibwa Indians in Canada's forested northland. It affects mainly males who have spent time hunting unsuccessfully for food in the frozen forests. Initially the subject feels morbidly depressed and nauseated, and experiences distaste for ordinary foods. He may have periods of semistupor. Gradually, he becomes obsessed with the paranoidal belief that he is bewitched, and he is subject to homicidal and suicidal thoughts. He feels that he is possessed by the Wiitiko monster, which is believed to be cannibalistic. As the psychosis develops, he begins to see those around him as fat luscious animals which he desires to devour. Finally, the subject enters a stage of violent, homicidal cannibalism. The Indians believe that if the subject reaches this point he is incurable and must be killed.

Parker noted that genetic predisposition, organic malfunctioning, and idiosyncratic traumatic factors in the life history may contribute to the "causes" of the disorder. However, he focused on the environmental pressures interacting with the Ojibwa personality which give rise to the syndrome.

The Ojibwa child is at first handled permissively and indulged, but between age three and five a drastic change occurs. The child is weaned from his dependency and prodded to assume adult responsibility. He is hardened by such practices as being made to run naked in the snow, he is goaded by the adult males to become a hunter, and he is taught by his mother to trap animals. By age nine, he has his own hunting grounds, and by age twelve he is a competent hunter, staying away for long periods, hunting in the silent frozen forests. The boy is made to fast until eventually he can go for long periods with only one meal a day. Punishment is often a matter of withholding food. Finally, at puberty, he is sent out into the forest without food and expected to remain there until he is able to communicate with the supernatural by means of a vision.

Parker summed up the important results of this experience as follows: (1) the procedure of indulgence followed by harsh dependency weaning leads to the development of covert dependency cravings; (2) there is a close association of food, eating, and self-esteem, wherein to be hungry is an expression of defeat and shame; (3) power, acceptance, and affection are secured by self-denial and suffering; and (4) security and self-esteem are vulnerable and must constantly be reaffirmed by external symbols of success.

As adults, the Ojibwa are characterized by a high level of interpersonal hostility, an indirect way of expressing this hostility, hypersensitivity to insults, exaggerated pride, and a paranoidal tendency.

The Ojibwa's childhood experiences lead to unsatisfied dependency cravings and repressed hostility. However, the societal structures do not allow acceptable outlets for these needs, and the adult Ojibwa treads a narrow path between his quest for affection and his desire to give vent to his rage. Failure in hunting can easily lead to pathological symptoms. Failure to obtain food threatens starvation and loss of self-esteem. The paranoidal feelings may result from the belief that one's bad luck is a result of others' practicing magic against one, a belief which develops easily in men who have repressed hostility. Failure as a hunter is a stress which leads to a breakdown of the normal defense mechanisms. Rage and aggression are then expressed in a direct and overt manner, rather than being turned inward as depression. In the full-blown Wiitiko psychosis, the symptoms of homicidal cannibalism serve to allay dependency cravings by becoming one with the object of the dependency (through eating it) while simultaneously aggressing against this frustrating object (by killing and devouring it). The cultural belief in the Wiitiko monster symbolizes the wide circle of significant others (especially the parents) who continue to frustrate the dependency cravings of the adult and who constitute threats to his self-esteem.

It is notable that a moderate case of Wiitiko psychosis is successfully treated by having other people prepare a dish of melted bear grease and berries which the patient drinks. This action simultaneously lessens hunger by providing a good many calories (important in the old days when the long winters were stressful for the Ojibwa) and satisfies some dependency cravings since the person is being fed and cared for by others as he was when a child. There may also be some significance in the choice of bear grease since bears are considered by the Ojibwa to be magically important animals.

Political homicide in Acan, Mexico

In the village of Acan, in the Tarascan area of Mexico, there have been seventy-seven homicides in the last thirty-five years, in addition to several hundred woundings and small arms exchanges. The population of Acan is only some 1,500, which means that the homicide rate is some fifty times greater than in the United States—about 200 per 100,000 per year. The majority of the homicides in Acan are motivated by political reasons and are considered as justifiable by the inhabitants of Acan. In fact, the homicide is often seen as obligatory by both the killer and the population of the town.

Friedrich (1962) has explored the Aceños' beliefs which lead to these views on homicide. It appears that political homicide is definitely legitimized by some of their views on human nature. Aceños see man as basically passionate with strong emotions that may at times be justifiably expressed. Those men that are susceptible to rages are at other times softspoken and polite; they are not undercontrolled aggressive individuals (see chapter 15). It is felt that every man needs a certain number of intimate friends. These compadres are often chosen politically and ritualized as intimates during the baptism of the children.

The Aceños also believe that all interpersonal relationships necessarily involve ambivalence. A man may love and be loyal to, and at the same time hate and envy his compadre. To kill because of envy is seen as a justifiable political act. Furthermore, men are seen as egoistic and brave, and it is felt that they must demonstrate their valor from time to time. The connection between personal emotion and politics is made by the belief that men are basically political.

Since men are not expected to be sadistic, homicide must be quick and painless in Acan. Also, since agricultural work is important to Aceños, men must not be killed while working or while going to and from their work in the fields.

Women are seen as outside these affairs. Thus, it is considered bad to kill a female, and on the whole women and children are not murdered in Acan. As a result of this, the Aceña women can sometimes be more outspoken than the men.

The Aceños are intensely political. Some 30 percent of the community are inactive, and some 50 percent are so involved that they compete for office and become embroiled in political homicides. Some fifty to seventy men are the most active core group. The town has been divided into two main political families for most of recent history. Whenever there is a coalition and a single party is formed, the party soon splits. Whenever a third party tries to form, it is quickly assimilated by one of the major parties or else is exterminated. Acan has five political families, but only two parties are prominent at any one time. Politics is geared to the prevailing social interdependency. Political homicide leads to vengeance, and killings because of vengeance lead to political reactions.

There are strong feelings that only Aceños should murder Aceños and 95 percent of the homicides have been within the Acan group. However, occasionally it is decided that a relative, compadre, or member of one's own party must be removed. Even though such political homicides are not avenged, members of the party may be unwilling to kill one of their own. Thus, though this is rare, an outside killer may be hired for the task. However, such homicides are not accepted as easily as interfactional killings.

Interestingly, most of the killings do not occur at the highest echelons of the parties. To attack the leader of the other party endangers one's own leader. Much of the killing, therefore, is carried out at the middle and lower echelons between persons with relatively few kin and compadre ties.

In spite of this interfactional fighting, the Aceños believe in community solidarity. They want the villagers to live together in peace. Both factions justify the killings in the interest of reuniting the town under one party. On one occasion in the past, two factions both claimed to represent the ex-president of Mexico, Lazaro Cardenas, and fought each other in the name of the same principles. Lazaro Cardenas, who knew the leaders of the factions, intervened personally to stop the killings in 1947.

In spite of this intent to restore peace and unity to the town, the political homicides continue. It is taken for granted in Acan that individuals succumb to homicidal passions once tensions have passed a given point. However, homicide is never viewed as the end; it is accepted only as a means. Friedrich (1962) quoted one leader as saying: "So we enter politics, we kill, and so forth. What else can you do?" (p. 327).

Culturally sanctioned homicides

The three societies we have just discussed covertly sanction homicide by providing institutionalized ways in which it is to be committed. Many primitive societies have gone farther and provided overt approval for culturally defined nonculpable homicides. A few such nonculpable homicides exist in Western culture, for example, the policeman who kills in the line of duty and the public executioner. Other societies have given broader approval to some types of homicide.

Bohannon (1960) noted two ways in which a society can institutionalize nonculpable homicide: in the jural or legal area and in the ritual area. In many African societies today, some forms of homicide are sanctioned and may be considered akin to lawful execution in the Western world. Thieves were often informally executed among the Tiv and the Alur, and they are occasionally so disposed of still. (Of course the European governments in the past treated these executions as nonculpable homicides.) The killing of witches was often considered nonculpable and also justifiable. Killing an adulterer was not considered by the Gisu or Luyia to be culpable. The Gisu considered homicide provoked by certain insults to be nonculpable; the Soga defended their right to kill in self-defense; and the Luyia considered killing for revenge to be nonculpable.

Ritual homicides are best illustrated by the practice of ritual sacrifice. In nineteenth-century Dahomey and Ashanti, human sacrifice was generally used as a means of executing criminals, though slaves might also be sacrificed. Among recent examples of this kind of homicide are the Mau Mau killings in Kenya. If one accepts African definitions, ritual homicide is not uncommon, although by European definitions it is rare.

There are also occasional institutional practices that involve the risk of homicide. The Tiv carry out a communal hunt with poisoned arrows which is recognized to be dangerous. Some 17 percent of Tiv homicides occur in the course of this practice. (The number of deaths among American hunters suggests a similar institution.) Homicides sometimes occurred at dances like those of the Alur, which were attended by rival groups, and ritual precautions were taken to guard against untoward incidents. (Again *West Side Story* presents us with a Western parallel.)

Part 3

Suicide and homicide

Chapter 11

Murder by suicide and suicide by murder

When a murder is committed, one generally expects people to condemn and criticize the murderer and to pity the victim who has died an involuntary and untimely death. When a suicide occurs, a single individual is seen in the roles of self-murderer and of victim, but public opinion generally stresses the fact that he has killed and is therefore to be condemned. One occasionally, though rarely, hears condemnation of a murder victim—for example, the statement that his death was his own fault because he should have had sufficient sense to avoid a particular person or place. It sometimes happens, too, that someone other than a suicide will be seen as his real killer, as when it is suggested that another person "drove him to suicide."

In the present chapter we are going to examine

149

these two relatively unorthodox ideas about murder and suicide: that a suicide may actually be a murder (a death brought about through the intervention of a second person) and that a murder victim may seek his own death.

Murder by suicide: psychic homicide (mental illness)

Hostile feelings toward others, even toward the most beloved friends and relatives, are present in everyone. Each person simultaneously has impulses of anger and hatred toward those dear to him and is surrounded by the hostility of those who love him. Yet it is almost invariably love which wins out, in spite of the occasional clashes and quarrels between those close to each other. For a few individuals, however, the hostility of family or friends may amount to murderous wishes which are expressed subtly or overtly. If the person who is surrounded by family hostility is particularly susceptible, he may succumb to a need to act out the wishes of his intimates by killing himself. Meerloo (1962) has described a typical case of this kind of acting out.

> An engineer who had struggled all his life with a harsh, domineering and alcoholic father gave his father a bottle of barbiturates to "cure" his addiction. He was very well aware of what he expected his father to do. When two days later the telegram came announcing the death of his father, he drove home at reckless speed, without, however, killing himself. Only after having gambled away his father's money did he come into treatment, but he was never willing to face his psychic murder. [P. 94]

There is other evidence that the families of suicidal people are hostile toward the suicidal one. Rosenbaum and Richman (1970) explored this problem with family interviews. Whereas the family member who had attempted suicide was often quiet during the interview or blamed himself, the rest of the family was usually reproachful and critical. For example, in one of their cases,

> One 17-year-old girl ran away with her boyfriend; when she returned home she became involved in a violent altercation with her parents, after which she swallowed her mother's tranquilizers. When seen in the hospital the mother angrily told the interviewer that she would find her daughter's death easier to bear than the strain she was being put under. The daughter reported that her boyfriend was so ambivalent and hostile that she told him, "If you want me to die why don't you say so?" [P. 1654]

Of course, this case involves the behavior of a family after the suicide attempt has occurred. Ideally, it would be best to study family patterns of behavior before any suicidal behavior took place. The suicide attempt may arouse a good deal of hostility which was not overt earlier. The family members may not know what to do with the suicidal person and may attack him because of the anxiety aroused when their incompetence is revealed. They may interpret his suicidal wishes as a rejection and criticism of them and be moved to counterattack. Or they may feel disgraced by his suicidal behavior and be angry with him for bringing shame on the family.

In the same vein, one may wonder to what extent the suicidal person's everyday behavior invites hostility and rejection, or to what extent the suicidal person is motivated to perceive others' feelings as rejecting. Rosenbaum and Richman said that their subject reported that her boy friend was so ambivalent and hostile that she asked him, "If you want me to die, why don't you say so?" If her description of the boy friend was correct, one wonders why she became involved with someone who was so blatantly hostile. We might note, too, that many people of only moderate hostility might become quite angry with an individual who habitually made melodramatic remarks of the kind quoted by Rosenbaum and Richman.

In spite of the criticisms we have just given, it is evident that suicides sometimes occur with considerable encouragement on the part of the suicidal person's loved ones and that such deaths may be considered as analogous to overt murders. However, we would suggest that the phenomenon of *psychic homicide* is more complex than simple acting out of others' hostility. The psychic killers may want the victim to die, and he simultaneously may want them to die. They in turn may feel the need to be involved in an ongoing sadomasochistic relationship of this kind. Relationships which carry the potential of psychic homicide may be carried on with mutual satisfaction for many years until some event causes the psychic killer to go too far or the suicidal person to become too susceptible.

Suicide by murder: victim-precipitated homicide

When murders are investigated, it is frequently found that the victim played an important part in bringing about his own death. He has, in a sense, committed suicide, using another person as his weapon. Suicide through provocation of murder has been given the name *victim-precipitated homicide*.

The proportion of victim-precipitated homicides is rather startling. Wolfgang (1957, 1969) investigated 588 homicides which occurred in Philadelphia between 1948 and 1952 and found that 150 or 26 percent of them had occurred after direct provocation by the victim. In many cases, the victim started the quarrel or was the first to show or use a weapon.

> For example, a husband had threatened to kill his wife during several violent family quarrels. He would usually later admit his regret for having beaten her and for having suggested the idea of her death. In the last instance, he first attacked her with a pair of scissors, dropped them, and then grabbed a butcher knife from the kitchen. In the ensuing struggle, which ended on their bed, she had possession of the knife, and there was considerable doubt in the minds of the jury whether the husband invited his wife to stab him or deliberately fell on the knife. In another case a drunken husband, beating his wife in their kitchen, gave her a butcher knife and dared her to use it on him. She claimed that if he should strike her once more she would use the knife, whereupon he slapped her in the face and she fulfilled the promise he apparently expected by fatally stabbing him. [Wolfgang, 1969, p. 92]

What sort of victim precipitates his own murder? He differs from the murder victim who is judged not to have provoked his own murder, and he is also different from the person who kills himself. Racial differences are apparent here. In Wolfgang's study, about 80 percent of victims who precipitated their murders were black, while blacks made up 70 percent of victims of ordinary murders. A larger difference is apparent when murder victims are compared to suicides: 90 percent of those dying by suicide were white.

A large majority (94 percent) of victims who provoked homicide were men. The majority of deaths from ordinary murder and from suicide were those of men too, but the proportions were smaller: 70 percent and 77 percent respectively. The murderer was much more likely to be a woman in victim-precipitated homicide (29 percent) than in ordinary killings (14 percent).

Victims who precipitated their murders have more frequently been drinking than victims who did not provoke the act. Perhaps the influence of alcohol played a part in the victim's provocative behavior. Excessive drinking can be seen as self-destructive behavior which would be in character with provoking murder. Alternatively, it could be that the effects of alcohol prevented the victim from defending himself as he might otherwise have done.

Precipitation of the murder by the victim was more common in slayings of spouses. In the victim-precipitated deaths, 22 percent involved spouses, while 15 percent of other murders involved mates. When the murder of a spouse was precipitated by the victim, the dead person was the husband rather than the wife in 85 percent of the cases. The husband was killed in a much smaller number of the husband or wife homicides which were not precipitated by the victim—only 28 percent. Perhaps this is the case because a man can threaten or attempt physical violence on his wife, frightening her into killing him, while it is less likely that a woman would be in a position to do so.

Wolfgang speculated that a husband who provokes his wife to kill him has unconsciously selected a mother substitute as the agent of death. This idea may have some relevance to the high proportion of blacks in victim-precipitated homicide, since it has been suggested that the mother in a black family is a more important figure than the mother in a white family.

Police records show that victims who precipitated their own murders had been arrested more often than those who did not. This was true even when crimes of assault alone were considered. In contrast, the killers who were provoked by their victims were less likely to have been arrested than those who killed spontaneously.

The victim who provokes his murderer is more likely to belong to the lower than the upper socio-economic classes. Assaultive behavior is more socially acceptable and more common in lower-class than in middle- or upper-class groups. Wolfgang has suggested that the kinds of aggressive acts to which a person is accustomed produce his cultural definition of appropriate ways to die. For lower-class black men, particularly, suicide may be seen as an unmanly and weak death, while dying in a fight is considered an admirable way to die. When the individual wants to die (presumably because of pressures which could produce suicide in a member of another group), he may unconsciously seek out a potential murderer and behave so aggressively that he is killed.

With reference to the idea of victim-precipitated homicide as a form of suicide, we might suggest that such a death is a peculiarly hostile form of suicide. It has often been hypothesized that suicide is a way of expressing rage; this would seem especially true of victim-precipitated homicide. First, the victim-to-be shows anger in the initial provocation of a potential murderer. Second, if a fight occurs prior to the murder, aggressive impulses can be expressed through blows. Finally, although the victim is probably not consciously aware of the fact, his choice of death almost guarantees that the murderer will be punished by imprisonment or death—the result, in this case, of the victim's rage.

Chapter 12

Homicide
and suicide

Why would anyone suspect that there was a relationship between the apparently different acts of suicide and homicide? The popular mind conceives the murderer as a vicious, unprincipled person with little sympathy for others. The suicide, on the other hand, is thought of as an introspective, esthetic, supersensitive person who kills himself because he thinks too much. The information given in this book indicates that the first picture is rarely an accurate one; the same is true of the second. Abandoning these common ideas about murder and suicide, we now ask whether the two could be similar in some ways.

Two general approaches have been taken to the problem of murder and suicide. Each of them suggests some predictions about the occurrence of each act. One important theory suggests that both murder and suicide are expressions of the same kind of aggressive impulse. The difference between them is that the murderer has learned to direct his aggressiveness outward, while the suicide has been taught to turn his inward—to attack himself, more or less seriously, when he feels the need to aggress. This theory (Henry and Short, 1954; see also chapter 16) says that people who direct their aggression outward do so because they were punished physically as children. Physical punishment meant that, if they retaliated against the parent, they might be spanked more, but they would not risk losing the parent's affection. Suicides, on the other hand, were psychologically punished, according to Henry and Short. The parent reacted to misbehavior by withdrawing love or attention. The child was then afraid to retaliate because a counterattack might mean permanent loss of the parental affection upon which he was so dependent.

Another, less detailed, approach to the question of the relationship between murder and suicide suggests that murder, suicide, and many other forms of deviant behavior are likely to occur at high rates among certain groups of people because of social factors leading to general unorthodoxy of behavior.

How can one tell which—if either—of these two theories is correct? Murder and suicide are both relatively rare behaviors. The number of individuals who commit both acts is still smaller. The study of the relationship between the two is thus not a simple thing. We will discuss two ways in which the relationship has been investigated.

Ecological correlations

The correlational approach involves studying a number of groups of people and seeing to what extent a high suicide rate is accompanied by a high homicide rate, and with what frequency the suicide rate is high while the homicide rate is low (or vice versa).

One investigator, Palmer (1965), collected information on a group of nonliterate societies and had judges rate them for the frequency of homicide and of suicide. He found that the two behaviors were positively related—societies with a high homicide rate also had a high suicide rate, while a low homicide rate was accompanied by a low suicide rate. Palmer had predicted that certain kinds of societies would have low suicide rates and high homicide rates. These societies would be the ones which were closely structured—that is, had a strong stress on mutual rights and duties. Palmer defined the closely structured societies as the ones in which crimes in general were severely punished. Contrary to his prediction, though, Palmer found that as the severity of punishment increased, so did both the suicide rate and the homicide rate.

Another researcher, Porterfield (1949), found the opposite results when investigating suicide and murder in the United States. He found that states with low suicide rates tended to have high homicide rates, while high suicide rates were accompanied by low homicide rates (that is, a negative correlation). When Porterfield examined individual cities within the states, he found some regional differences. In every nonsouthern city the suicide rate was higher than the homicide rate, but that relationship held for only eight of the forty-three southern cities. Porterfield noted that the cities with an average suicide rate had the highest homicide rates.

It is evident that researchers find different relationships between suicide and homicide depending on the size and type of the social group they are studying. The

French researcher, Halbwachs (1930), for instance, found evidence in one study for both a negative and a positive correlation between homicide and suicide. According to his study, the Catholic provinces of Germany had a high incidence of assault and a low incidence of suicide. The Protestant provinces had a high suicide rate and a low assault rate, while the mixed provinces had equal rates of both. However, in France, no such pattern emerged. There was a positive correlation between the suicide and assault rates in all provinces.

Porterfield (1952) tried to develop a concept which would help explain some of these differences. He suggested that the secularization of a society, the extent to which it differs from a folk society, may be an important variable. The folk society is the closely structured society we mentioned with reference to Palmer's work, a society in which there are many external constraints on behavior and much stress on interpersonal ties. A secular society, in Porterfield's definition, is one in which there is a loosening of neighborhood, friendship, and kinship ties, where there is a breakdown in mores, and where relatively few of the inhabitants are indigenous. In this sort of society, Porterfield predicted, there should be a high suicide rate and a low homicide rate. This prediction was supported when indices of secularization and the rates of suicide and homicide were correlated for the states of the United States.

Unfortunately, there seem to be some studies which raise serious questions about the validity of all of these correlational studies. David Lester (1971) has reported data that indicate the arbitrary nature of sociological correlations between behaviors. He correlated the suicide rate and homicide rate of societal groups over time, dwelling area, and status categories, and computed these correlations for each sex and racial group also. The correlations that resulted from these procedures varied enormously. The correlation over years for the United States was positive, the correlation over the states was zero, and the correlation over a status category (age) was negative. The correlations over states for white females and white males were both positive. The correlation over states for nonwhite males was negative, and for nonwhite females it was not significantly different from zero.

Lester felt that his results clarified the discrepancy between Palmer's finding of a positive ecological correlation between homicide and suicide and Porterfield's finding of a negative correlation. The correlation reported by Lester for the total population was not significantly different from zero. This absence of a correlation is probably the most likely state of affairs.

Lester concluded from his data that sociological studies of the relationship between suicide and homicide using correlational techniques were of limited use. The choice of which particular type of correlation to use (temporal, ecological, status) introduces an arbitrary factor into the research. To look at all possible types of correlation (and to look at them for different subgroups of the population) reveals the full complexity of the association between homicide and suicide. Lester doubted that any existing theory was able to predict the various correlations satisfactorily. The most fruitful way to investigate the relationship between homicide and suicide may be to use psychological and sociopsychological techniques to study differences in the *individuals* concerned. How do murders who subsequently commit suicide differ from nonsuicidal murderers and non-homicidal suicides? What are the personality, constitutional, and developmental factors that influence the choice of behavior?

Comparisons of individuals

Pokorny (1965) looked at self-directed and other-directed aggression, when complete and when partial, by examining data about murderers, people who assaulted others (but did not kill them), completed suicides, and attempted suicides. He examined differences in place of occurrence of the act, the census tract of residence, the hour of day and month of the act, the age of the individual, the race of the person, and the sex of the person. He found that the murderers were similar to the assaulters in all characteristics; they tended to be young, black men living in poor neighborhoods. The murderers and the completed suicides differed in all characteristics except that of sex, since the completed suicides were most frequently older white men. The completed suicides differed from the attempted suicides in hour and day of act, age, and sex. (Young women were especially common in the sample of attempted suicides.)

Pokorny concluded that homicide and suicide are committed by different types of people. Attempted suicides appeared to be a mixed group. They resembled the completed suicides in place of occurrence of the act, their race, and the census tract in which they lived, but they resembled the murderers in the hour and the day of the act and in age. They were different from the other three groups in the high proportion of women among them.

Pokorny's work is all that seems to be available on the topic of individual differences between suicides and murderers. However, it suggests strongly that people who commit suicide differ from those who commit murder. On the whole, those who direct their aggression outward do not also turn it inward, and vice versa. The ethnic and social class differences noted by Pokorny suggest that inward or outward direction is not determined by innate differences, but rather by experience. Differences in child-rearing practices within social subgroups may well be responsible for the direction of aggression.

The suicidal murderer

Some murderers, of course, kill themselves immediately after their crime. Pokorny's evidence about the differences between murderers and suicides suggests that these people are unusual cases and may be of some interest.

The frequency of suicide after murder varies considerably from country to country. In England, one study (West, 1966) found that 33 percent of murderers subsequently killed themselves. Wolfgang's (1958) study in Philadelphia found that only 4 percent of murderers there did so. Because of this difference, a good deal of the information available about suicidal murderers comes from England.

West compared suicidal murderers with a group of nonsuicidal murderers and found that the suicidal ones were more often females, were older, more often killed victims who were close relatives, used gas and shooting more, and tended to kill earlier in the week and more often in midsummer than the nonsuicidal murderers. They had fewer criminal convictions than the nonsuicidal murderers. The two groups did not differ in marital status (except that the nonsuicidal group had an excess of single males) or in the time of day for the murder.

Two important factors in the pattern emerge from these data. First, the suicidal murderer is on the whole a different kind of person from the nonsuicidal murderer. He is much more likely to be killing a spouse or child and is less likely to use brutal methods such as strangulation, blows, stabbing, or a blunt instrument. Gas and shooting are more frequently used, and these methods are distinguished by the fact that they involve killing at a distance. This makes sense when one remembers the close relationship between many suicidal murderers and their victims, which may inhibit the killer from carrying out his act brutally or in a way which requires close observation of the dying person.

Secondly, the suicidal murderers lie between the nonsuicidal murderers and the nonhomicidal suicides in their characteristics. Only 12 percent of the nonsuicidal murderers were females while women made up about 40 percent of the suicidal murderers. About 39 percent of the completed suicides in England are women. In age, the suicidal murderers were somewhere between the younger age range typical of murderers and the older age range typical of suicides.

West concluded that the suicidal murderer was representative of the general community, unlike the nonsuicidal murderers, who were more often single males and from the lower classes. He found that the suicidal murderers were neither all insane nor all sane. The proportion of offenders with psychiatric disturbances was roughly the same as that in the nonsuicidal murderers. Little evidence in this study indicates that the suicidal murderer killed himself in order to avoid punishment. The large number of infanticides, possible death pacts, mercy killings, and possible accidental killings may indicate that a large number of the suicidal murderers were motivated by feelings of despair rather than hostility. In other cases, there appeared long-standing histories of violent and suicidal behavior. West felt that a large number, though by no means all, of suicidal murderers were individuals with a high level of aggression which may turn against others or themselves according to the circumstances. The following is a case of a typical suicidal murderer reported by West.

> The offender was an excitable, talkative, boastful man of low intelligence. He was constantly unemployed on account of symptoms of backache, which were considered by hospital doctors to be largely hysterical. He was referred to a psychiatrist and put on a tranquilizer. He was in severe conflict with his wife, and various authorities had been approached to intervene on account of his violence toward her and his children. He was described by a family doctor as "a pale little man, full of resentments against the world and immensely aggressive." He so resented interference that when his baby had pneumonia he turned out of the house the doctor who called to examine the child. He was reported to have been so irritated by his baby crying during a fatal illness that he picked it up and threw it across the room. His wife had been seen by social workers badly bruised and with a

tooth knocked out following arguments with her husband, and on another occasion he had attacked his wife in a very frightening way in the presence of a social worker who had called about the children.

Six weeks before the murder, the offender's wife finally left the home, and two children remained behind. He made numerous threats that unless she returned he would kill the children and himself. Finally, he did so, leaving behind a note blaming his wife. [PP. 83-84]

West felt that suicidal murderers resembled completed suicides more than murderers, and he concluded that homicidal-suicidal acts were extensions of suicidal acts. The suicidal individual is likely to be as angry and outwardly aggressive as the nonsuicidal person. If one accepts the theory that the typical suicide is a frustrated murderer (Lester and Lester, 1971), it is quite conceivable that the aggression might spill over and manifest itself in outwardly aggressive acts, even to the point of murder.

Wolfgang (1958) investigated a group of American murderers who killed themselves after their crime. His results led to conclusions similar to those of West. The suicide occurred soon after the murder is most cases, and the victim was much more likely to be a relative or lover in the case of the suicidal murderers. Contrary to what West discovered in England, however, Wolfgang found that in Philadelphia the suicidal murderers were more likely than nonsuicidal murderers to be males and that they were more likely to be brutal in their killing. Wolfgang attributed the excessive brutality to a greater reservoir of frustration and anger, but the factor of the sex of the killer must be taken into account before this conclusion is accepted. West's English suicidal murderers used less violent methods and were predominantly female.

Wolfgang also noted that the suicidal murderers were older, more often white, and their victims younger than in the case of the nonsuicidal murderers. The suicidal murders were more likely to take place in the home and the killer and victim were more likely to be of opposite sexes. Alcoholic intoxication was less common in the suicidal murderers.

Wolfgang suggested that the two possible reasons for some murderers' killing themselves after the murder, excessive frustration and guilt, were difficult to demonstrate. However, he noted that the murderers who killed themselves were less likely to have records of arrests than nonsuicidal murderers and that this perhaps indicated a greater degree of law abiding and conformity to the social mores. Thus, the notion that guilt or the desire to escape punishment may be responsible for the subsequent suicides of murderers may have some degree of validity.

Another investigator, Dorpat (1966), looked at eight cases of American murderers who completed suicide after killing their victim. His data supported those of West. The suicide followed closely upon the murder. There was an intimate but discordant relationship between the murderer and the victim, and the murder frequently followed real or threatened separation. The murderer was frequently found to be psychiatrically disturbed. Dorpat suggested that the threat of separation led to regression of the ego to an undifferentiated phase of psychic development in which there is fusion of the self and object. In this state the aggression can be directed at either the self or the significant other. Dorpat also felt that murder-suicide represented an acting out of reunion fantasies.

Wolfgang (1958) looked at a group of wives who killed their husbands and a group of husbands who killed their wives. He found that ten of the fifty-three husbands subsequently completed suicide whereas only one of the forty-seven wives did. He hypothesized that husbands were more likely to precipitate their deaths by provoking their wives (by beating them, for example), so their wives felt less guilt after murdering them than the uxoricidal husbands did after their acts. The husbands' feelings of guilt would make suicide more probable, while the wives would feel that their acts had to some extent been justified. Wolfgang noted, in support of his hypothesis, that twenty-eight of the murdered husbands were classified as victim-precipitated homicides whereas only five of the murdered wives were so classified.

Theoretical propositions

Some problems in the study of suicide and homicide have given rise to theoretical suggestions which have not been adequately tested. The theories are intriguing, however, and we are going to discuss them briefly because they may contribute to the fruitfulness of the reader's thinking.

One problem has to do with racial differences in homicide and suicide rates. The nonwhite homicide rate is the highest, the white homicide rate is the lowest, and the white and nonwhite suicide rates are in between. In order to explain this pattern, Lalli and Turner (1968) used the concept of open and closed societies (which are comparable to Porterfiled's secular and folk societies). An open society is one

> made up of classes in which the achievement, rather than the ascription of status is emphasized, rational solutions to problems are sought, personal decisions and personal freedoms are prized. [In contrast] . . . the closed society is a tribal, caste or estate social system in which taboos and conventions are held in high regard. Ascriptive status spells out nearly all the rights and duties of the people [Lalli and Turner, 1968, p. 196]

In order to explain the pattern of suicide and homicide rates discussed above, Lalli and Turner suggested three plausible assumptions: (1) In a social system made up of an open society with a closed society in tow, the open one will direct violence inward, the closed one outward; (2) the rate of the typical form of violence in the open group. Also the rate of the atypical form of violence in the closed group will be higher than the rate of atypical violence in the open group; and (3) the rates of violence will increase as class decreases.

The basic assumption made by Lalli and Turner, of course, is that white American society can be considered an open society while black American society is necessarily classified as a closed society. This idea is difficult to accept. The black's behavior is fixed by his ascribed status only with reference to some situation within the white society. In his relations with other blacks, he possesses earned status and prizes personal freedom as much as whites do.

Another problem found in the study of suicide and homicide has to do with the effect of economic change on the frequency of the acts. Henry and Short (1954), whose ideas we discuss more fully in chapter 16, tried to deal with this issue.

They attempted to show that suicide rates rise during times of economic depression and fall during prosperity whereas homicide rates fall during depression and rise during prosperity. Homicide was seen as characteristic of low status individuals and suicide was seen as characteristic of high status groups. Their data provided partial support for their ideas. Suicide and homicide, for Henry and Short, were acts chosen by different individuals. In looking at the reasons for choice of suicide versus homicide, Henry and Short discussed the role of the degree of external restraint in the society over the behavior of the members of the society and they also looked at the role of frustration and the psychological factors (such as the strength of an individual's superego) that affect the aggression consequent upon this frustration.

Henry and Short argued that as the economy improves, low status individuals lose relative status compared to high status individuals. This generates frustration, and the aggression in low status individuals is directed outward. Hence homicide increases in frequency during prosperity. During depression, the high status people lose status relative to the low status people and this generates frustration for them. The aggression consequent to frustration in high status people is directed inward. Thus, suicide increases in frequency during depressions.

Although Henry and Short saw homicide and suicide as opposing choices, they did discuss the reason why murderers might have a high suicide rate. Since murderers often murder close relatives and these close relatives may have been a former source of nurturance, Henry and Short argued that there is a resulting inhibition of aggression and internalization of the values of the source of frustration. These processes would tend to inhibit the future outward expression of aggression consequent to future frustration and so the tendency to direct aggression against the self is increased. They added that, having internalized the values of the source of frustration, after the loss of nurturance the self becomes a legitimate target for aggression.

The problem with this line of reasoning is that a tendency to inhibit future aggression consequent to future frustration does not seem relevant to murderers who kill themselves soon after their act of murder or at the same time. It does not seem relevant to murderers who kill themselves after killing their infant children, or relatives who are not sources of nurturance. Further, there does not seem to be a logical reason why murderers should internalize the values of their victim.

Henry and Short hypothesized that those who kill themselves after murdering someone are probably individuals with strong superegos who have internalized societal prohibitions against the outward expression of aggression. Clearly, however, the prohibitions were not sufficient to prevent murder in the first place. Perhaps the strong superego is present together with impulsive tendencies or perhaps these murderers resemble Richard

Solomon's dogs. Solomon (Mowrer, 1960) found that if he punished dogs before they committed some act that had been classified by Solomon as forbidden, they were resistant to temptation, but when they did commit the act they showed little emotional reaction (the analogy of guilt in humans). If the animals were punished just after they began committing the forbidden act, they were less resistant to temptation, but after committing the act they showed much more emotional disturbance. The study of the punishment process in children who later become murderers might be of interest.

Conclusions

It is almost impossible to come to a decision about the relationship between suicide and homicide on the basis of the information which is presently available. There is no conclusive evidence that murder and suicide are opposites, nor is there much evidence that they are acts with a similar function. Perhaps the problem is that the relationship between suicide and murder can be understood only within a particular culture or sub-culture. In some groups of people, attitudes may be such that suicide and homicide are alternatives; in other groups, suicide and homicide may frequently be committed by the same people. (One may note the differences between studies done in America and in England). Hendin (1969) has noted that among young black men suicide is often considered a particularly cowardly act, while participation in murder, whether as killer or as victim, is seen as a manly way to behave. In other groups, a suicide is regarded with pity, but a murderer with abhorrence. To consider suicide and murder outside a cultural context is to act as if the behaviors were things in themselves, as if a murder had the same meaning, motivation, and consequences whether it was committed in Westchester County or among the Tiv of Africa. Such an assumption, we suspect, is based upon notions (like those of Freud) that all aggressive acts are fueled by an instinctive motivation which is the same for any human being. Perhaps, at some level, that concept of aggression is true. However, it does not seem to provide a fruitful approach for studies of the relationship between various destructive acts.

Part 4

Why people kill

Chapter 13

The well of anger: theories of violence

Theories about homicide have the same purpose as theories about any complex human behavior: organization of information into an understandable form, with the hope that a particular way of organizing will help researchers understand what questions to ask next. The universe in its raw form is too chaotic for humans to grasp. They must pick out a few observations and deal with those as best they can, formulating ideas about the basic ways in which the material of the observations is interrelated. Because human minds are limited, theories about human behavior are often rather simple. This fact should become apparent to the reader in the present chapter. The theories we discuss will generally deal with biological, psychological, or sociological factors in homicide. Rarely do theorists attempt to bring all these data together; they themselves would be unable to grasp a theory complex enough to include all possible factors. Thus, the reader should approach the theories described below as what they are, tentative attempts to begin a solution of a complicated puzzle. They are not attempts to tell the Truth with a capital T. They contain many guesses and many "unproven" hypotheses. They also contain some illuminating ideas about the nature of murder.

BIOLOGICAL BASES FOR MURDER

Genetic Factors

It is quite evident that aggressiveness in lower animals is strongly influenced by heredity (McClearn, 1969). Mice with particular genetic backgrounds are ferocious, whereas other mice with different heredity are tame. This genetic influence is clear when one compares wild rats with laboratory rats, which belong to the same species but which have been carefully inbred. Wild rats will attack the gloves of anyone who tries to handle them and often tear through them with their teeth, while the laboratory rat can usually be picked up easily by a barehanded laboratory assistant.

To demonstrate that human violence is affected by heredity is more difficult since, of course, one cannot do selective experimental breeding on humans or isolate children from their parents in order to make sure that results are due to heredity and not to learning. Genetic abnormalities are somewhat easier to study, and it has recently been suggested that some murderers may have chromosomal aberrations. The normal male has a sex chromosome arrangement which is called XY, with the

X chromosome coming from the mother and the Y chromosome from the father. The normal female carries XX, with an X chromosome coming from each parent. These arrangements occur because the XY chromosome pair of the normal father's reproductive cell splits, producing a set of sperm of which half carry the X and half the Y chromosomes. The mother's cells split too but all ova carry the X chromosome since that is the only sex chromosome that she carries. When the father's and the mother's genetic material combine at fertilization, only the combinations XX and XY normally occur. However, in rare cases, either sperm or ovum may carry sex chromosomes which did not split properly. As a result, the offspring will have an aberrant sex chromosome makeup.

Two abnormal sex chromosome arrangements are thought to play a possible role in violence. Occasionally one finds males who look physically normal except for undeveloped testes, but who actually have three sex chromosomes instead of two. One variety have XXY (which is known as Klinefelter's syndrome). These men are sterile, occasionally mentally retarded, and have an unusual proneness to aggressive behavior. It has also been found that among tall male criminals there is a high incidence of the genetic abnormality XYY. There are no good estimates of the frequency with which this genetic aberration occurs among tall noncriminal males, but some workers, like McClearn (1969), have concluded that this genetic abnormality does seem to be associated with criminal violence.

Thus, there are probably some genetic influences on human violence. We have at present no understanding of the mechanism which might be at work, linking a genetic arrangement to violent behavior. Some of the brain dysfunctions which we will discuss below are possibilities for the role of the mediating factor, as are some hormonal processes.

Phylogenetic factors

One approach to human behavior involves the study of behavior in lower animal species who are thought to be most closely related to man — who shared a common ancestor with man in the course of evolution. In recent years, ethologists (zoologists who specialize in a particular method of studying animal behavior) have documented the frequent occurrence of aggression among lower animals (Lorenz, 1966). Almost all animals will show frequent aggressive behavior, particularly in defense of their personal territory or home, where they allow no intruders. Man's closest animal relatives, of course, are the chimpanzees, baboons, gibbons, and other primates. The primates are almost all strongly territorial animals, which will fight to eject any stranger from their property. They also have a strong motivation to establish dominance relationships, or a pecking order, within their group, and will fight or at least bluff with the object of establishing exactly who's who. Ardrey (1961) has suggested that humans are descended from a group of apes with strong aggressive and killing tendencies, and that they therefore possess instinctive needs for aggression which must be satisfied in one way or another.

Although lower animals are strongly aggressive and will fight a great deal under the right circumstances, killing of a member of the same species is much more common among humans. One reason for this may be that in modern times man has developed killing methods which do not give the victim time to make a submissive gesture, or which operate at such long distances that he cannot be affected by the way the victim looks and acts. Even in medieval times, when killing was usually effected by the short-range methods of knife or lance, humans had elaborate rituals which allowed surrender rather than death. Now death can be delivered by means which involve little or no contact with the victim, and surrender is not a real possiblity. When a pilot drops bombs on a village he has never seen before, he cannot be affected by the submissive gestures of the victims; nor does he consider asking them to become his prisoners rather than bombing them.

However, even leaving aside the problems of killing at a distance, man aggresses against man, and has always done so, in a manner more sadistic than that of any lower animal. Some human beings are capable of slowly torturing others to death in spite of their close proximity and their excellent view of the submission of the victim. Perhaps humans have to some extent lost instinctive inhibition of aggression in response to a victim's behavior. Or perhaps other factors are involved – the tendency of humans to live in more and more crowded conditions (which lead to increased aggressiveness in other species), or, of course, the fact that so much of human behavior is learned.

Brain disease and injury

Disturbing the functions of the brain and central nervous system can have many effects on human behavior – paralysis of the limbs, loss of the ability to speak, loss of concern about the future, and so forth.

Aggression, too, seems to be affected by nervous functioning. Experimentation with subhuman animals has emphasized certain parts of the brain as involved with violence. The area which appears most responsible for aggressive behavior is the so-called limbic area of the brain, a primitive part of the nervous system which lies buried between the two halves of the cortex. If a part of the limbic system is given a mild electric stimulation, the animal will respond by aggressive movements. (The animal feels no pain, we may add, and aggressive behavior does not follow stimulation of most other parts of the brain.) If the area where stimulation brings about aggression is later removed, the result will be an animal which is tame and can hardly be instigated to aggression. Similarly, removal of the limbic areas in epileptic humans has been found to reduce their aggressive behavior (McClearn, 1969; Ervin, 1969).

In humans, at least, excessive aggressiveness could be caused by a second problem other than a defective limbic system. Other parts of the cortex probably work to control the limbic system and prevent direct expression of anger, even when the person has been seriously annoyed. Diseases which cause degeneration of the brain would remove this control and allow uninhibited expression of aggressive urges.

There is some support for the idea that abnormal brain functioning can be connected with aggressiveness in humans (Ervin, 1969). Brain damage, caused by a blow, by hemorrhage, or by a tumor, often leads to a personality change which may include increased aggressiveness. Patients being treated for episodic dyscontrol (see chapter 15) often show signs of brain dysfunction when the brain's activity is measured by electroencephalogram. Studies of criminals, too, have shown that they are more likely to have abnormal electro-encephalograms than are noncriminals.

This last statement applies to murderers and to others who are habitually aggressive. Williams (1969) compared the EEGs of murderers, habitually aggressive delinquents, and the general population. The first group (in which Williams included attempted murderers) showed abnormal brain functioning in 24 percent of its members. The habitually aggressive delinquent group showed abnormal EEGs in 64 percent of its members, while abnormal EEGs occurred in only 12 percent of the general population. The fact that the murderers, although they were more often abnormal than the general population, were not nearly as often abnormal as the habitually aggressive delinquents, suggests that a good deal more than brain dysfunction is responsible for the frequency of homicide. In particular cases, however, brain dysfunction may have a great deal to do with the occurrence of a specific murder. One group of criminals, those who have an abnormal sex chromosome arrangement, has been found to show an excess of abnormal EEGs (Fenton, Tennent, Comish, and Rattray, 1971), which suggests a mechanism by which genetic abnormalities could cause an increase in aggressiveness.

A number of murderers and attempted murderers who had abnormal EEG patterns have been reported. Matthew and Constan (1964) described a patient with abnormal brain rhythms (14 and 6 per second spiking, a syndrome which is thought to be common in murderers). Their patient was an eighteen-year-old white male who had experienced a normal birth, but had fractured his skull at the age of six months when he fell from his high chair. Although his weaning and toilet training were accomplished at normal times, he did not speak until he was three years old. Throughout his childhood, he complained of headaches, which he tried to soothe by putting cold wet towels against his head. Similarly, he complained about his eyes, but optometric testing showed that he did not need glasses. His school work was poor and the teachers considered that he did not apply himself; he quit school in the tenth grade.

His first seriously aggressive behavior occurred as the result of a trivial incident. His father asked him to turn the television off and he refused. The argument developed into a fight, with the two throwing things at each other. The son tried to choke the father and the mother had to separate them. Later, he threatened the father with a gun, saying that he hated him and had thought of killing him.

When he was eighteen the patient joined the Air Force, but within five weeks was given a medical discharge and advised to seek psychiatric help. His records stated that he was emotionally unstable and had made a suicide attempt, though he himself claimed that he did not know why he had been discharged. After the discharge, he avoided his friends and spent a lot of time watching television and movies. One day he threatened the family with a gun and fired shots at the doors and windows. He threatened the police when they came, but was talked into surrendering. Later, in the hospital, he said that he hated his father and sister, that he had often felt suicidal, and that he heard voices telling him things. He said he disliked having to live by society's laws and wished he could have lived in the Old West or among gangsters.

The precise relationship between the abnormal brain rhythms and the aggressiveness in Mathew and Constan's patient is, of course, uncertain. The boy seems to have had an unusually low tolerance for frustration, perhaps because of an inability to cope with complicated situations. The latter disability is characteristic of brain-damaged patients. However, one should ask whether some characteristic of the environment also predisposed him to aggressiveness. Was the fall from the high chair an unusual incident, or was it evidence for a general carelessness with the child? If the parents generally took many chances with their son's safety, this could mean that they may have felt quite hostile toward him, thus producing an atmosphere which would foster aggressiveness. The father seems to have been rather aggressive himself; most men would not begin to fight and throw things at a disobedient child. The boy's aggressiveness might well have been learned at home rather than caused primarily by his abnormal brain functioning.

Drugs: can they cause violence?

There is a strong popular belief that the use of the common "recreational" drugs is causally associated with violence. However, according to Ervin (1969), the use of marihuana, narcotics, psychedelic drugs, amphetamines, or tranquilizers does not increase aggressiveness. The individual under the influence of these drugs is no more likely to be homicidal than he is when not on the drugs. Of course, criminal activity and violence may be associated with obtaining the drug. Assaults and murders may occur in desperate attempts to get enough money to buy the desired drug, but that is a completely different phcnomenon from violence activated by the influence of the drug.

There is, however, some evidence that alcohol and antidepressant drugs may cause an increase in violence in some people under some circumstances. Whether all people are potentially susceptible to these effects is not clear. Perhaps susceptibility is related to the presence of certain brain dysfunctions which become apparent only when cortical functioning is impaired by alcohol or the like.

Hormones and violence

Bodily functions and behavior are strongly influenced by hormones — chemical substances which circulate in the blood and penetrate to every part of the body. The sex hormones in particular are known to be strongly related to aggressiveness in lower animals. The male sex hormone, testosterone, has a strong influence on the aggressiveness of animals. People have made use of this information for centuries in the practices of castrating male horses in order to gentle them and male calves so they will grow fat and be easy to handle. A neutered male housecat appears in strong contrast to the uncastrated tom; while the tom generally has mangled ears or even a missing eye, the other avoids fights and remains sleek and unscarred. The female animal is generally much more gentle and avoids severe conflict with man and with her own species alike. Under the influence of the hormone prolactin, however, she may become quite dangerous. Prolactin is secreted after the young are born, during the suckling period. In general, the aggressiveness of a female at this point is directed toward the protection of her offspring.

The role of the sex hormones in human aggression is unknown. That the presence of testosterone might be responsible for the greater incidence of violence in men as compared to women has been suggested.

The hormone insulin, which is concerned with the use of sugar by the body, has been slightly implicated in aggression. Apparently hypoglycemia caused by excess insulin sometimes leads to aggression in man. Again, however, this may occur only in individuals who already have some tendency to lose control over their aggressive tendencies.

PSYCHOLOGICAL BASES FOR MURDER

Megargee (1969) has suggested that there are three separate psychological components at work in violence: the strength of the motivation toward aggression, the internal inhibitions which work against aggression, and the environmental or stimulus factors which facilitate aggression. In this section, we will look at information about each of these components in turn.

The instigation toward aggression

The psychological theories proposed by Freud contributed one important idea which is used today in considering aggressiveness. He postulated that man acts because of two major groups of instincts or motivations: the life instincts (Eros) and the death instincts (Thanatos). The aim of the death instinct is the destruction of the individual—an idea developed by Freud after seeing the carnage of the First World War. The life instinct, of course, opposes self-destruction, and a compromise between the instincts is reached by turning aggressiveness outward toward other people. Thus, in the thinking of Freud's most orthodox followers, a tendency to self-destructiveness is primary and other-directed aggression is secondary. Some less orthodox psychoanalysts do not accept the idea of death instincts. They feel that aggression is caused by frustration of the organism's needs, and that other-directed aggression is primary.

The psychoanalysts who accept the idea of death instincts (and the ethologists, whom we discussed earlier) consider aggression to be an innate, inherited trait, which has always been and will always be characteristic of human behavior. Some theorists feel that aggressiveness is not innate, but is triggered off under the influence of particular environmental pressures. The best known of these environmentalist theories is that of Dollard, Doob, Miller, Mowrer and Sears (1939), which is known as the frustration-aggression theory. According to this idea, aggression arises only when the organism's needs are not satisfied. Aggression is always a consequence of frustration, and the amount of aggression which occurs is highly related to the amount of frustration which is present. The animal which is deprived of food for two days is more likely to attack than the animal which has been deprived for only one day.

Dollard et al. did not include in their theory any judgment as to whether the connection between frustration and aggression had to be learned or whether it was innate. That there are other possible consequences of frustration besides aggression is evident. For instance, frustration can lead to fixation or regression in behavior rather than aggression. That leaves two possibilities for the frustration-aggression connection: it may be inborn or it may be the result of experience.

An alternative environmentalist theory of aggression is a social learning theory approach. In this theory, the tendency to be aggressive is thought to result from particular child-rearing practices, from the behaviors a child is rewarded for, and so on. These learning experiences lead the person to develop a particular way of responding to situations. The urge to aggress can be part of his response style.

Inhibition of aggression

No person, be he gentle or violent in manner, aggresses every time the mood strikes him. When he does aggress, his style of attack varies with the situation; sometimes it is a minimal expression of hostility like a sarcastic remark, other times it involves the all-out aggression of a death struggle. Each person, then, must have some inhibitions which control his aggressiveness.

As we noted earlier, theorists like the ethologists who hold that the urge to aggression is innate also feel that there are innate inhibitors of aggression. These range from ritualized behaviors to submissive postures which prevent a more dominant animal from attacking.

Eysenck (1964) has suggested that both inherited and learned factors may be at work in the control of aggression through inhibition. He proposed, unarguably, that people differ in the ease with which they learn. This statement has special reference to the primitive form of learning at work in the development of conditioned responses — associations between the perception of some stimulus and some automatic response to it. In Eysenck's conception of the process, people who have inherited an excitable central nervous system learn conditioned responses readily, while those whose nervous systems are dominated by inhibitory processes do not. Eysenck suggested that inhibitions against aggression are learned, and that, therefore, the person with an inhibitory nervous system will learn inhibitions less well and be more aggressive than the person whose nervous system is excitatory. He predicted that murderers and other criminals should learn conditioned responses more slowly than noncriminals.

Social learning theory assumes that the environment alone governs the development of inhibitions against aggression. The methods used in socializing the child determine whether he will inhibit or express his impulses toward aggression.

Stimulus factors

Although no one has elevated stimulus factors to the status of a theory, it is quite obvious that they can serve as essential determinants of the occurrence and nature of an act of violence. They may be part of the situation which instigates violence, as when a person provokes another into attacking him. They may help to inhibit aggression; intrafamily violence, for example, is often considered a private act, and husband and wife may refrain from attacking each other in the presence of outsiders. The availability of a weapon may determine the extent of damage done to another person since one cannot stab without a knife or shoot without a gun. It is, indeed, possible that the presence of a weapon could serve as an instigator to violence. This is the assumption made by groups which are lobbying for gun control laws with the object of reducing violence in the United States.

SOCIOLOGICAL BASES FOR MURDER

Theories which derive the causes of violence from sociological factors deal, of course, with social systems and not with individuals. Although the social systems are made up of individual people, these subunits of the system are not of interest to the sociological theorist as they are to the theorist who feels that individual functions are at the root of violence. Schrag (1969) described the following sociogenic theories of violence.

The subculture theory

The theory that subcultural differences are responsible for violence suggests that the goals and strategies of particular subcultures may well differ from those of the major or normative groups of the society. In order to conform to the style of his subculture, an individual must behave deviantly with respect to the norms of the society as a whole. Wolfgang and Ferracuti (1962), in fact, proposed that some subcultures may normally include behaviors which are considered unusually violent according to societal norms. For people belonging to such a subculture, violence is the expected response to a jostle, a derogatory remark, or the appearance of a weapon in someone's hand. Deviation from the violent norm will lead to punishment as surely as does deviation from the nonviolent norm in the normative society. The nonviolent person in the violent subculture can expect to be ostracized or even punished with violence.

Wolfgang and Ferracuti think it is possible to use certain indices to identify which groups in this society are subcultures of violence. They have suggested using the homicide rate for this purpose. For instance, black

males of ages 20-24 would be noted as a violent
subculture because they have the highest homicide rate
— 92.5 per 100,000 per year. Unfortunately, Wolfgang
and Ferracuti ran into a problem of circularity here, as
they noted themselves. If they used the homicide rate to
identify violent subcultures, they could not then use the
idea of a violent subculture to explain why a group has a
high homicide rate. They suggested that one way to
solve the problem might be to use indices such as rape,
aggravated assault, or recidivism to identify subcultures
of violence. Then the concept of the violent subculture
could be used to explain the high homicide rate.

The value of the subcultural theory is hard to judge
at this point. It seems to be little more than a
restatement of the fact that some groups direct aggression outwards more than others do. The theory does not
attempt to explain why subcultures of violence arise.
The reasons probably lie in factors such as child-rearing
practices in a culture. In any case, to have much
explanatory power, the theory should suggest links
between other characteristics of the subculture and the
fact that it is a violent one.

Opportunity theory

Another approach which stresses the differences
between subcultures is opportunity theory. Rather than
considering differences in subcultural norms, the theory
deals with the fact that society allocates rewards and
penalties, opportunities and restraints, differently to
different subgroups. In industrialized societies, particularly, there is an uneven distribution so that some
groups become relatively disadvantaged. The disadvantaged persons can increase their rewards by

legitimate means, but illegitimate means such as crime and graft are often more readily available to them. The people who become involved in crime often get their training and make their work easier by joining gangs. Opportunity theory is particularly interested in the question of gang membership. It suggests that those who turn to crime and join gangs do so because they feel alienated from the legitimate normative system and feel they cannot make it legitimately. This feeling may stem from the belief that they lack ability or contacts or luck, or that they will meet with prejudice because of racial membership or physical handicaps. According to opportunity theory, then, violence arises primarily because some segments of the population feel they are denied an equal slice of the pie.

Status incongruence theory

One theory attributes violence to conflict among the various roles a person can take. Each individual may act in a number of different ways — as man, husband, father, Presbyterian, Rotarian, employer, and employee. If his roles involve little conflict, they are said to be congruent. In the case above, for example, there is no reason why a Presbyterian should not marry and have children. If there is conflict or incongruence among the roles, the person will probably suffer discomfort, stress, and anxiety. One could turn the congruent list of roles into an incongruent and conflicting one, for instance, simply by changing "Presbyterian" to "ordained Catholic priest."

Status incongruence is most likely to be strong when a person shifts roles in a society. The cartoon strip "Maggie and Jiggs" depicts a family which is dealing with role incongruence following a shift in economic role from lower-middle to upper economic class. Jiggs deals with the incongruence rather well since the roles most important to him (pub crawler and *bon vivant* of Duffy's bar) can be maintained in the face of other role shifts. Maggie, on the other hand, is under constant stress because her new role as lady of culture is not congruent with her role as Jiggs' wife. Gibbs and Martin (1964) have argued that suicide is more likely when much status incongruence is present. Maggie has not yet gone that far although she is certainly much more violent than Jiggs.

Social disorganization theory

The approach called social disorganization theory looks at ways in which a social system's healthy functioning can be disturbed by epidemics, wars, or migrations, for example. Such disorganization may cause the norms of the society to come into conflict with one another. For example, in the case of a severe epidemic like the Black Plague, there was a conflict between the usual norm of giving prompt and dignified burial to the bodies of loved ones, and the new normative behavior of avoiding all contact with the bodies of plague victims. The individual cannot possibly conform to all the norms since they are in conflict with one another. The resulting deviation from norms and breakdown of social customs and expectations may lead to further deviations from the societal norms, including increased violence.

Of the theories we have examined in this chapter, many were not formulated with the intention of explaining murder alone. Instead, they were intended as general theories of aggression. Although research has been done to test the theories, many of them have not been examined for their applicability to murderers and to murder. However, there do exist some theories which have been especially considered for their relevance to the phenomenon of murder. Also some data exist about which little theorizing has been done but which suggest the hypothesis that there are two distinct kinds of personalities to be found among murderers.

The theories and the data of special importance for the study of murder need to be examined in some detail. For that reason we have not discussed them in this chapter, which needed to cover too much other material. The next three chapters will be devoted to consideration of three important topics. First, we will discuss a study which dealt with the frustration aggression hypothesis as it relates to murder. Second, we will examine some work which implies that there are two distinct kinds of murderers. Third, we will talk about a special form of social learning theory.

Chapter 14

Frustration, aggression, and murder

The frustration-aggression hypothesis of Dollard et al., in addition to other theories of human violence discussed briefly in the previous chapter, leads to rather more complicated theorizing. We shall examine the theory in greater detail now.

Dollard and his colleagues postulated that aggression is always a consequence of frustration. Frustration arises when some barrier prevents a person from satisfying a drive or need which has been aroused. The barrier may be a matter of the individual's lack of competence or the physical environment may present barriers so great that even a competent person cannot overcome them.

Ordinary life is filled with unavoidable frustrations from birth onward. The infant's activity is restricted by clothing and by his crib, as well as by his natural limitations. He is weaned, toilet trained, and moved toward independent behavior. The process of growing up involves countless minor and many major frustrating episodes. To adults, the environment presents frustrating obstacles in the tasks of earning a living and getting along with other people. Loved ones are lost through death and separation, frustrating the desire to continue the relationship with them. And at the end of life is the final frustration of all, the loss of all known satisfactions through one's own death.

Not all of the frustrations we have just noted are responded to by aggression. Other possible responses are regression, a change to less mature behavior; repression, putting the frustrating situation out of awareness; and fixation, persistent maladaptive behavior. Our interest, of course, is in the aggressive result of frustration, and the factors which determine whether a frustrating episode will result in aggression or in one of the other behavioral possibilities.

Dollard et al. felt that the occurrence of and strength of aggression were determined by the degree of frustration and the strength of the restraints against aggression. The restraints may involve a fear of punishment which might actually occur, or, alternatively, a fearful feeling which is related to past experiences rather than to any real future punishment.

In addition to asking what factors determine the occurrence or nonoccurrence of aggression, one needs to ask how the *direction* of aggression is determined. An aggressor can turn his hostility either outward toward other people or inward upon himself (through suicide, self-mutilation, or long-term self-destructive behaviors like alcoholism). One factor which may determine the direction in which aggression is turned could be the individual's degree of socialization — the extent to which he has learned to follow willingly the cultural norms for behavior. If the child is oversocialized and he follows too strictly the cultural restraints against outward-directed aggression, he will learn to inhibit his aggressive behavior and perhaps turn it inward upon himself. If, on the other hand, he is not taught to conform to the social strictures about aggression (that is, if he is undersocialized), he will be rather directly aggressive toward others when he is frustrated. Moderate socialization will permit outward expression of aggression in acceptable ways — verbal rather than physical aggressiveness, professional or athletic competition rather than fistfights, displacement of anger toward some other object (for instance, pounding the table) rather than striking the person one is arguing with.

Any child meets with frustration in frequent moderate doses. But what happens to a child who is severely frustrated — denied affection by his parents, physically tormented, or made a social outcast? Such a child feels a great deal of anger and resentment toward those who frustrate him. However, he may not be permitted to express his anger in any way, especially if the parents do not teach him socially acceptable ways of showing aggression. If this is the case, he may develop a vast reservoir of suppressed (or even repressed) aggression. Eventually he will grow up and become free of parental restraints. Then, even minor frustrations may trigger off the release of all the anger built up through the major frustrations of his childhood. Moreover, since the individual has not learned the skills which allow most people to express aggression in small, socially acceptable doses, either he will suppress his anger until it becomes uncontrollable, or he will use socially unacceptable ways of aggressing which lead to punishment and further frustration.

Palmer (1960) investigated a group of murderers with the intention of testing some of the implications of the frustration-aggression hypothesis. On the basis of the reasoning about severe frustration which we gave in the preceding paragraph, he argued that murderers should have two characteristics. First, they should have experience of a great deal of frustration as children. Second, they should have failed to learn socially acceptable ways of expressing aggression.

In order to test his ideas about murderers, Palmer used the excellent technique of comparing the murderers to their brothers, who had never committed murder. He identified a sample of fifty-one murderers, all of whom had nonmurdering brothers. To find out about the murderers' childhood experiences, he interviewed them and their parents. This method, of course, might have led to some distortion in the information, since the parents knew which son had committed a murder and which had not. That is, a parent might be influenced by his knowledge of the murder to think of all the unfortunate events in the murderer's life and none of those in the life of the other son. Palmer felt that the parents' reports were fairly accurate, however. He could check them to some extent by comparing them with his interviews with the murderers.

In his interviews, Palmer investigated the frequency of physical frustrations in the murderers' childhoods, the frequency of psychological frustrations, and the extent to which the murderers were taught to release aggression in a socially acceptable fashion.

Physical frustration

Palmer found a number of aspects of physical frustration, many of which occurred in significantly different amounts for the murderers and their brothers.
1. *Difficult births:* Twenty-eight of the fifty-one mothers reported that the birth of the murderer had been difficult, while only nine considered the birth of the control brother a difficult one. In addition, the mothers felt that the pregnancy, the labor, and the weeks immediately after the birth were more difficult in the case of the sons who later murdered than in the case of the brothers. This suggests two sources of stress for the murderers: first, the effects of the difficult birth on the child himself, and second, a chain of negative attitudes toward the child set up in the mother by the difficult birth circumstances.
2. *Forceps injuries.* In nine of the murderers but none of the brothers, forceps were used with severe external effects. These included torn mouths, lacerated ears, and indentations of the skull. Four of the nine defects were permanent and visible in adulthood.
3. *Serious operations in childhood:* The murderers had a total of nineteen surgical operations in the first twelve years of life while the brothers had a total of four. The operations included appendectomies, operations on the genital organs, and heart surgery. There was no difference in the frequency of circumcision or the age at which it was done.
4. *Serious illnesses in childhood:* The murderers had a significantly greater number of serious illnesses in the

first twelve years of life than their brothers did. There was an unusually high incidence of epilepsy, severe measles, pneumonia, and whooping cough among the murderers.

5. *Age at illness:* Of the severe illnesses mentioned above, more occurred at an early age among the murderers than among the brothers. Eleven of the murderers had a serious illness in the first year of life, while none of the brothers did.

6. *Serious accidents:* Twenty-three of the murderers but only six of the brothers had serious accidents during childhood. It was especially notable that thirteen of the murderers and none of the brothers fell on their heads. (Palmer, incidentally, noted that the falls tended to occur in the presence of the mothers, as if they allowed them to happen. One mother, whose son had fallen down a long flight of stairs, said, "I put the carriage by the head of the stairs because it was hot and there was a nice cool breeze there and I didn't think it would tip over" [Palmer, 1960, p. 75].)

7. *Beatings by others:* About three times as many murderers as brothers were beaten severely once or more by people other than their parents.

There were, of course, some physical frustrations which did not differentiate the two groups.

8. *Starvation and suffocation:* There were no differences between the murderers and their brothers in the frequency of the traumatic experience of starvation or suffocation.

9. *Beatings:* There were no differences between the murderers and their brothers in the frequency of beatings by the mothers or in the age at which these beatings occurred. However, the fathers tended to beat

the murderers more often than they beat their brothers.

In examining the total differences in physical frustrations, Palmer assigned a point for each physical frustration an individual had experienced. The murderers had an average of 4.5 points, while the brothers averaged only 1.7. In forty of the fifty-one pairs, the murderer had the higher physical frustration score, in seven pairs the scores were equal, and in four pairs, the brother had the higher score. The murderers on the whole had thus experienced more physical frustration than the brothers.

Palmer presented the case of a boy who at the age of eighteen murdered a middle-aged prostitute with whom he had just had intercourse and whom he was trying to rob. Mike, the boy, reported the following experiences when Palmer interviewed him. He was constantly beaten as a child. When he was five years old, his uncle got angry with him and threw him across the room so that he hit the stove. His two older brothers once beat him with sapling branches until he was covered with welts and bleeding, after which he was unconscious for two days. On several occasions his uncle put him under the hood of the car and started the engine. His uncle and brothers once gave him an electric shock just to amuse themselves. He recalled that his brothers had thrown him into a fast-moving stream on the pretext of teaching him to swim, with the result that he nearly drowned. The brothers also once tied a snake around his neck, causing him to "go out of his mind" for almost a week. Mike's mother added an anecdote which he did not tell Palmer: that his leg had been pierced by a homemade javelin when he was eight years old.

Psychological frustrations

Emotional as well as physical frustrations were more common among the murderers than among their brothers, as the following summary shows.

1. *Congenital deformities:* The murderers had a greater frequency of visible congenital defects (ten for the murderers versus two for the brothers). These included an abnormally large head, club feet, abnormal eyes, and a badly twisted neck—all deformities which tend to provoke social reactions. Such defects can give rise to social ostracism and consequent psychological distress, particularly during childhood.

2. *Postnatal physical deformities:* Visible defects acquired after birth (for example, facial scars and crippled limbs) were also more common in the murderers (fifteen versus five). Such defects, like congenital deformities, lead to social problems. The difference between the murderers and their brothers becomes even more apparent when one combines the numbers of congenital and acquired defects: twenty-six of the murderers were afflicted in comparison to only seven of the brothers.

3. *Maternal attitudes:* Prior to the murderers' births, fourteen of the mothers were unhappy about the coming child, while only four mothers reported unhappiness about the prospective births of the brothers. Undoubtedly, a negative attitude toward a child can begin long before the child is born, particularly if the child was unwanted or the pregnancy is difficult. When such an attitude continues after the child's birth, it is bound to be communicated to him and to result in emotional frustration.

4. *Maternal rigidity:* The mothers' treatment of the murderers tended to have been less flexible and less responsive to the children's needs than their treatment of the brothers. For instance, the murderers were more often fed on a fixed schedule than on a self-demand schedule. The result of such treatment is likely to involve a greater amount of psychological frustration than is the case when childrearing is tailored to a child's needs.

5. *Toilet training:* Toilet training was more likely to have been started in the first year for the murderers than for the brothers. In addition, the murderers were more likely to have experienced some extremes in toilet training: of the seventeen children trained within a month, ten were murderers, and of the fifteen whose training took over a year, ten were murderers. Early toilet training can be a cause of psychological frustration for several reasons. First, the child may not be sufficiently mature to do what is being asked of him, and he will fail even if he is motivated to try. Second, the overeagerness of the parent often reflects the parent's greater consideration of factors other than the child's needs (for example, the parent's convenience or competition with the people next door). Extremes of toilet training, too, reflect sources of emotional frustration. Rapid training implies that severe methods are being used. A long time spent in training implies that the parent started before the child was ready, or was highly inconsistent, or turned the training process into a battle for authority.

6. *Sexual activity:* The mothers tended to have punished and suppressed sexual self-play earlier for the murderers than for the brothers.

7. *Maternal responses to the child:* When the mothers were annoyed with the children, they were more likely to respond to the murderers than to the brothers with anger, crying, or isolating themselves. Such responses would be sources of psychological frustration because handling them would be beyond the child's abilities. In addition, they serve to create distance between parent and child and to deprive the child of the maternal nurturance he needs.

8. *Verbal abilities:* The murderers were significantly slower than the brothers in learning to speak and read. These problems are to some extent symptomatic of psychological frustration and disturbance, but they can also be sources of frustration. The child who is slow to speak may be teased or belittled. He also is unable to express his needs as early as other children can. The slow reader is exposed to criticism and may be kept back in school, which alienates him from his own age group.

9. *School experience:* Twenty-three of the murderers as compared to five of the brothers said that they had disliked school. This suggests that the murderers tended to have frequent frustrating experiences since they were required to attend school, which was distasteful to them.

10. *Disturbed behavior in childhood:* As children, the murderers were more likely to have phobias, compulsions, persistent bedwetting, sleepwalking, and nightmares, and were more likely to stammer. Like the speed of learning to speak and read, these traits are simultaneously indices of disturbance and sources of further frustration. Stammering and bedwetting are particularly likely to draw frustrating attempts at correction from parents.

11. *Emotional control:* Temper tantrums and emotional outbursts were more frequent in the murderers than in their brothers at age five. Twenty of the murderers were reported to have had tantrums once a week or more, while none of the brothers were said to have lost control so frequently. Lack of emotional control could occur because the child was already so frustrated that some minor irritation was enough to push him over the brink. Depending on the parents' response to the outburst, the child could experience further frustration as a result of losing control.

12. *Lack of satisfactions:* The murderers spent more time alone than their brothers and were less happy with their work. Thus they were getting little satisfaction from two important sources of psychological support.

As in the case of physical frustrations, there were some psychological frustrations which were not much different for the murderers and their brothers.

13. *Parental marriages:* There were no differences in how the parents were getting along when the murderers and the brothers were born.

14. *Maternal solicitousness:* The mothers felt that they had responded equally quickly when the murderers and the brothers cried as infants.

15. *Feeding and weaning:* There were no differences in the frequency of breast or bottle feeding or in the age at weaning.

Assigning one point for each frustration, Palmer calculated an index of psychological frustration. The murderers averaged 4.7 psychological frustration while the brothers had an average of 2.5. When the physical and psychological frustration scores were combined, the average total frustration score was 9.2 for the murderers and 4.2 for the brothers.

Aggression release

As we have mentioned, a person can use socially acceptable outlets for aggression (verbal attacks, athletics, and so forth) or socially unacceptable outlets (stealing, fist fighting, and so forth). Unacceptable outlets are likely to lead to punishment and further frustration. Palmer investigated the use of acceptable and unacceptable outlets for aggression by the murderers and their brothers.

Among the possible acceptable aggression releases, the murderers less often used the following: verbal loudness at age five, verbal release of anger at age five, physical fighting at age five, dirtying clothes at age five, and athletics at age seventeen. More often than their brothers, the murderers used anger outbursts short of temper tantrums at age five.

There were no differences in the extent to which the groups talked back to their mothers at age five, hunted at age seventeen, or used verbal aggression at age seventeen.

Overall, then, the murderers tended to use fewer socially acceptable ways of aggressing than their brothers did. The average number of acceptable outlets was 2.4 for the murderers and 3.5 for the brothers.

As one might predict, the murderers tended to use more socially unacceptable outlets than the brothers did. They were reported as using: lying at age five, stealing at age five, temper tantrums during childhood, intoxication at age seventeen, and violent aggression while drunk at age seventeen. There were no differences in the frequency of swearing at age five or fist fighting at age seventeen.

Curiously, the murderers not only were more cruel

to animals than their brothers were, but also showed more solicitousness and care for animals.

The murderers thus tended to use unacceptable outlets for aggression more often (an average of 1.2 outlets for the murderers versus 0.4 for the brothers).

Since there are a number of acceptable ways of releasing aggression, why did the murderers not use them? Palmer speculated that the strong drives to aggress created by their excessive frustrations made the murderers fear that they would be unable to control their aggression if they began to allow its release. This created a vicious circle, since some aggressive release was imperative and appeared in forms such as temper tantrums. This unacceptable aggression led to punishment and further frustration, making it (according to Palmer) even more unlikely that acceptable outlets for aggression could be used.

Not all of Palmer's subjects were identical in their ways of showing aggressiveness though all of them had murdered. Some were ordinarily highly aggressive in unacceptable ways. Others had shown little aggressiveness other than the murder. When Palmer looked at the frustrations that each of these groups had experienced, he found that the aggressive murderers had had many more frustrations than their brothers. For the nonaggressive murderers, the number of frustrations was somewhat higher than for the brothers, but the difference was not statistically significant.

Discussion

Palmer's data confirmed the hypothesis that murderers have been subjected to an unusually great amount of frustration when they were children. The aggressiveness which was apparently produced by this frustration was never channeled into acceptable outlets but was released in undesirable ways. The majority of the murderers were in no sense professional killers, but they had killed while emotionally upset and frustrated. Often, they had killed people who resembled their early frustrators. For example, a man who had been beaten by his father beat an older man to death, while a boy who had been severely frustrated by his mother killed a middle-aged woman.

The two types of murderers whom Palmer described figure in the next chapter. One type of murderer, apparently nonaggressive and overly conforming, suddenly explodes into violence when frustrated. The other type is superficially well socialized but basically resentful and lawless. The work of Megargee, which we will discuss, attributes these characteristics of murderers to overcontrolled and undercontrolled aggressiveness.

Chapter 15

The control
of aggression

Thousands of detective stories invite readers to guess who committed a murder. Suspects can be identified by uncovering the *motive*—the reason for the killing, such as financial benefit or romantic revenge. In everyday life, however, many murders do not seem related to any of the motivations present in fictional killings. A large number of them are sudden murders, murders without motives. The murderer appeared normal up to the time of the murder. There was no reason for him to choose the person he killed rather than another victim. No premeditation took place, as the precipitating event occurred immediately before the killing. The murderer was not in the habit of using physical violence.

The reader will remember Palmer's suggestion that

some murderers are habitually aggressive, while others are quiet people who suddenly commit some tragic act of violence. The same idea has been developed by Megargee (1966), who classified murderous criminal behavior into two kinds: overcontrolled and undercontrolled, corresponding respectively to a quiet life followed by a brief orgy of aggression and to a consistent pattern of violent activity. Megargee described the two types of criminals.

The undercontrolled aggressive person has low inhibitions against aggression. Whenever he is frustrated or provoked in any way, his response is an aggressive one. He is not completely unable to control his aggression because he exercises some command over the specific types of aggression he commits and the persons against whom he directs the aggression. If there are specific strictures against attacking a particular person, such as a judge or a parent, he can easily displace his aggression to someone else. He does not aggress wildly, gouging eyes or wielding axes, but chooses somewhat more acceptable ways of attack. However, he is definitely undercontrolled in that he cannot inhibit aggression as completely as most people can. Thus, he is constantly involved in violent scrapes. Because of his minimal inhibitions against aggression, he is often diagnosed as a sociopathic personality.

The chronically overcontrolled person, on the other hand, has abnormally rigid controls against aggression. No matter what the provocation, it is unlikely that he will respond aggressively. His inhibitions are so general and pervasive that he cannot release aggression by displacing it or substituting a less drastic act than the one to which impulse might first lead him. He has little skill in allowing aggression to be expressed in small acceptable amounts which gradually release and dampen his rage. Instead, unreleased aggression, the fruit of a lifetime of minor frustrations, builds up until even more powerful controls cannot continue to inhibit it. When that point has been reached, some minor frustration is the last straw and brings about some catastrophic, completely inappropriate act of aggression. The model boy becomes a murderer, and no one can understand why. Mcgargee and Mendelsohn (1962) have commented about these people:

> The extremely assaultive person is often a fairly mild-mannered long-suffering individual who buries his resentment under rigid but brittle controls. Under certain circumstances he may lash out and release all his aggression in one, often disastrous, act. Afterwards he reverts to his usual overcontrolled defenses. Thus, he may be more of a menace than the verbally aggressive "chip-on-the-shoulder" type who releases his aggression in small doses. [P. 437]

In support of the ideas of the undercontrolled and overcontrolled murderer we can cite some research evidence. The research of Blackburn in England is in agreement with the dichotomy. Blackburn (1968a) tested criminals with the Minnesota Multiphasic Personality Inventory. The extremely assaultive criminals appeared to be more repressed and more overcontrolled than those who were convicted of crimes in which they were only moderately assaultive. In a second study, Blackburn (1968b) compared paranoid and nonparanoid schizophrenic offenders. The offenders who were judged to be extremely assaultive were not on the whole the ones who had been persistently assaultive. Most of the homicidal offenders had, in fact, no previous history of aggressiveness. As was the case for the criminals Blackburn studied earlier, those who appeared more repressed on psychological testing were more likely to have committed extreme assaults.

Some older concepts about murder are also relevant to the overcontrolled-undercontrolled concept. The idea of sudden murder—murder without a motive and without much previous conflict—seems strongly related to the style of the overcontrolled murderer.

The sudden murderer is a person who, without having been involved in any previous serious aggressive or antisocial acts, unexpectedly murders another. There is a single, isolated episode of violent, impulsive acting out behavior.

Weiss, Lamberti, and Blackman (1960) made a comparison of sudden murderers, habitual criminals, and sexual offenders. The habitual criminal offender fitted the classical picture of the antisocial psychopath who comes from a broken home with much overt hostility among family members. The person's insecurity has been handled by superficial bravado and extraversion, the blaming of troubles on others, and the acting out of infantile hostilities in a succession of crimes. The typical sexual offender, on the other hand, came from a family in which relationships were superficially warm, but in which the father was hostile or indifferent to the patient. There were problems in sexual identification and insecurities about sexual adequacy and general coping ability. The offenders were introverted, denied their conflicts, and drifted or were provoked into immature patterns of sexual acting out. The sudden murderer differed from both these criminal types in coming from a cohesive home, in which a domineering, overprotective mother emphasized conformity to the rules of the social system. When he failed to conform, because of his feelings of inadequacy and hostility, the patient blamed others and wandered around looking for greater opportunities. He felt consciously alone and isolated from others. When he began to get along better, he became more and more tense and angry because society expected him to become still more mature and provided him with no one to blame for his troubles. Provocation at this point could trigger a murderous rage.

Blackman, Weiss, and Lamberti (1963) described sudden murderers as young males whose fathers had been hostile, rejecting, overstrict, or indifferent. The killers were generally in good health and had IQs in the dull normal range and poor work records. The men maintained ties with their families of origin and had sex lives which were either inhibited or promiscuous. Their emotions were complicated by feelings of interpersonal inadequacy, confusion about sexual identity, and underlying feelings of anger and resentment. After killing, the sudden murderers assured their own apprehension by the police, confessed their guilt, and appeared bland, unconcerned, and self-righteous.

Ruotolo (1968) presented several case histories of sudden murderers. We will describe one of these.

Carlos had come to the United States from Puerto Rico when he was twenty-one. At the time of the murder he was twenty-six and worked as a laborer in a machine shop, and sent money home to Puerto Rico for his widowed mother and younger sisters. He had never been in trouble with the law and kept to himself. When he was twenty-five, he had met a girl in Spanish Harlem and brought her to where he worked as his common law wife (with her guardian's permission). The girl was not an expert housewife. Carlos had to instruct her in cooking and cleaning. His feelings for her alternated between pity and anger, depending on whether he saw her as stupid or defiant. He had hit her occasionally when he was frustrated. She accepted this passively. At one point he sent her back to Puerto Rico but he got lonely without her and recalled her.

His wife had two faults that particularly angered Carlos. First, she giggled when he berated her. Second, if any man treated her kindly or bought her an ice cream soda, she would reward him with sexual favors. Once Carlos hid and watched his wife go to a movie with a sixty-year-old man and neck with him during the movie. He confronted them and dragged his wife home. He beat her, blackening both her eyes. She seemed bewildered rather than remorseful. He then decided to take her back to her uncle (her former guardian) in New York. On the way to her uncle's he stopped at a deserted lot and had sexual intercourse with her, which she accepted passively. He bagan to feel remorseful for beating her and asked her for forgiveness but her response was one of incomprehension. Then he threatened to kill her. Although he could not recall why he did so, he thought that he may have been trying to get her to change her ways. He placed his hands around her neck but she said that he wouldn't dare to kill her and giggled. Then he strangled her. He lay beside her for a while and shook her, but she did not move. He went home and took a bath. The next day he went to the lot again and she was still there so he called the police anonymously. He was arrested the next day.

When interviewed after the crime by a psychiatrist, he eventually admitted to having seen his wife after her death. He said that he did not have proof that she was alive and that he did not plan to tell the judge that he had seen her. But some day he would find out and then he would be happy.

Carlos was not tried in court since he was judged insane (with a diagnosis of schizophrenic reaction) at the time of trial, though insanity at the time of the crime was not proven. A postmortem on his wife revealed a cyst in the frontal lobe of her brain which may have led to her intellectual deficit and emotional liability.

Carlos was a provider. In addition to his mother and his sisters, he supported a retarded waif. His interpersonal relations were shallow and he failed to recognize his wife's defects. He was neurotically committed to the Spanish idea of manhood which tolerates no infidelity in the wife. His assault on his wife met with minimal response from her. He tried to be self-effacing but here too he was rebuffed. His pride was hurt and he shifted back to manliness and threatened her. The conflict situation had aroused his anger too much for him to keep control and he murdered her. In his psychotic fantasy, he was able to reconstruct a relationship with his wife that he could not have in life, and his pride was restored.

Ruotolo felt that two significant events take place prior to sudden murder. First, the individual's pride is dealt a shattering blow which triggers self-hate. This anger often is transformed to the victim and abates after the murder. Second, the individual tries a new solution to his conflict which is too precipitous and unpracticed to be sustained. This triggers panic and anxiety. The individual tries to resume his previous neurotic solution and often annihilates the victim, who may inadvertently obstruct this shift back.

Ruotolo felt that the sudden murderer was often unaware of his own feelings, especially those of anger. "They were strangers imprisoned within their own skins and subjected to volcanic eruptions of unpredictable direction and force" (p. 174).

Evidently the sudden murderer suffers an abrupt and temporary loss of control over his aggressive impulses. Shortly after the homicidal act, he is his old self again—a mild-mannered, quiet person who will not even argue loudly, much less kill someone. Why this abrupt change? It seems hard to understand in view of the usual assumption that there is some continuity in people's ways of behaving. Perhaps some ideas which were put forward by Menninger and Mayman (1956) will be of help here. Although not specifically directed toward either, their ideas are relevant to the concepts both of sudden murder and of overcontrol.

The underlying assumption of Menninger and Mayman's analysis is that the individual is always doing whatever is the best thing he can do, given all the pressures and demands within him and all the conflicting demands of the environment. Being psychotic, for example, does not look like a satisfactory solution, but according to this viewpoint, it must be the most satisfactory way for the individual dealing with conflicts which are almost irreconcilable.

Menninger and Mayman particularly stressed the idea that as soon as the individual establishes some sort of equilibrium, new events require him to make a readjustment. They discussed four ways in which readjustment could produce a new (though temporary) equilibrium.

1. *First order methods* of readjustment include manifestations of anxiety such as insomnia, restlessness, and uneasiness. These symptoms help restore some equilibrium between the environment's demands and the individual's needs by forcing the individual to attend to his needs at the expense of those of the environment.

2. *Second order methods* of readjustment are more extreme expedients which are brought into play when the first order methods fail. They are commonly called neurotic symptoms or syndromes, and involve the individual's inability to perform some acts or a compulsion to do so. These symptoms protect the individual to some extent from the demands of the environment and make it possible for him to protect himself from conflicts. He pays the price of being handicapped by his symptoms, however.

3. *Third order methods* which take over when neurotic symptoms can no longer protect the person's equilibrium are of most interest to us in our study of murder. These methods were given the label *episodic dyscontrol* by Menninger and Mayman, who commented:

> But what more can an already stretched, over-taxed, wearied, exhausted ego do? The ego seems to "give way"; some of the dangerous primitive impulses whose pressure is so largely responsible for the tension, which all of the previously

described devices were designed to control, elude its restraints. They escape; they are enacted; they go toward targets and they wreak their destructive purpose. [P. 156]

The individual may obtain relief from his internal demands by violent aggression. But the consequences of such antisocial acts lead the person into further trouble. The episodic dyscontrol did not completely preserve the person's equilibrium, but it was not a bad compromise in a difficult situation since it at least protected him from psychosis.

Menninger and Mayman suggested that episodic dyscontrol is in some cases consciously organized and in other cases the result of unconscious motivations. The organized group would include the psychopath and the sociopath who consciously reject the norms of society and feel free to violate them at will. The disorganized, unconsciously motivated form of episodic dyscontrol would include brief psychotic attacks, attacks of panic and demoralization such as those which occur in battle, attacks of assaultive violence, and convulsions.

4. *Fourth order methods* of coping with stress are the psychoses, in which the individual can no longer cope with the demands of the environment and withdraws into fantasies, delusions, and hallucinations.

Discussion

The work of Megargee, of Ruotolo, and of Menninger and Mayman seems to confirm the existence of a type of murderer who is not habitually aggressive—who, in fact, is abnormally quiet and controlled. Rather than throwing his weight around at the bar every Saturday night, he is a model boy or model husband who, once in his whole life, commits a serious act of violence, after which he returns to his normal quiet behavior. These ideas raise a number of social questions.

For one thing, perhaps one should be concerned with teaching children to express aggression appropriately rather than concentrating on the inhibition of anger. At the present time, many parents who are concerned with the achievement of world peace may, in line with their general philosophy, discourage their children from fighting, even if they are attacked. The opposite extreme is the parent who feels that the child, especially if a boy, must always fight back and not let himself be pushed around. This approach to childrearing could lead to undercontrol of aggression and a tendency to try to solve all problems by means of aggressive acts. The other approach, although it appears to teach peaceful cooperation, might if carried to extremes lead to overcontrol and a real inability to deal with aggressive impulses. In order to provide a child with optimal control of his aggressive needs, one might best concentrate on teaching him to use socially acceptable ways of expressing anger—to encourage verbal expression of anger and displacement methods like competitive games. Whatever one's theory of the source of aggression, at present the great majority of humans seem to have strong aggressive impulses. Until a way to short-circuit these is found, people need safe ways to release them.

A second question of social importance has to do with society's treatment of the murderer. Whatever one's approach to this problem, to use the same standards in dealing with the overcontrolled as with the undercontrolled murderer may not be appropriate. If his past behavior is a good predictor (and it is probably the best predictor one has), the undercontrolled killer is going to go on getting into major and minor violent scrapes if he is permitted to do so. The overcontrolled murderer is most likely to live his quiet life, although if he does lose control again the results are likely to be serious. The answer one gives to the question of society's treatment of the murderer depends, of course, on whether one perceives the appropriate societal response to be punishment of the murderer or the protection of other members of society.

Chapter 16

Stresses
of society

So far, we have dealt primarily with the influence
on murder of personal events in an individual's life, such
as parental absence or mistreatment. Sociological
theorists take some interest in such events, but they are
also concerned with the effects on homicide of conditions in the larger society. Some influential conditions
could be war, change of governments, or the economic
states of inflation and depression. Before discussing
theory, we will review some of the sociological factors
associated with murder.

Some sociological correlates of murder

Quinney (1965) found that the homicide rate was
low in countries where urbanization and indus-
trialization were relatively great. The high rate of

homicide in rural, nonindustrialized countries, Quinney felt, was due either to socialization of individuals in a subculture that stresses violence, or to poor education, lack of sophistication, and a limited frame of reference.

Porterfield (1958) found that in the United States homicide was negatively correlated with alcoholism, socioeconomic status, suicide rate, lung cancer, and cirrhosis of the liver. Both Porterfield (1949) and Quinney found slight negative correlations between the homicide and suicide rates. In eighty-six cities, those in the South had a higher homicide than suicide rate, whereas cities outside the South had a higher suicide than homicide rate. Over the years from 1910 to 1946, the rates changed in opposite directions during times without crises, but during crises they changed in the same direction. During the World Wars both rates went down, and during the depression both went up.

Pettigrew and Spier (1962) studied Negro homicide in states in which there was a large proportion of blacks in the population. The homicide rate of blacks was higher where there was a higher proportion of blacks born out of state, and where the white homicide rate of the black's home state and state of current residence was higher. There was no association of the homicide rate with socioeconomic status or family disorganization variables. It was concluded that there were two kinds of states in which the black homicide rate was high: where the blacks had a highly homicidal subculture with rapid social change in progress, and where there was a moderately homicidal culture with high nonwhite migration (especially from states with a high homicide rate).

Rudin (1968) studied developed nations and found

that deaths from murder, suicide, and alcoholism were statistically associated. He hypothesized that these deaths reflected a societal orientation of aggressiveness and acting out. He felt that the societal need for power (as measured by the Thematic Apperception Test) would correlate with the nation's death rates from suicide, homicide, and alcoholism. The data only partly supported his predictions, the need for power being correlated only with the suicide rate. Lester (1967) found the same association for a sample of primitive societies.

Barrett and Franke (1970), in another study of developed nations, pointed out that social and medical variables are more likely to influence death rates than are societal motives. They found that the homicide rates of developed nations were associated with the status integration of the society, a measure of the degree to which individuals in a society are in the roles expected for people of their sex, race, and age.

Only one major theory about homicide has been developed within the sociological framework, that of Henry and Short (1954). In this chapter, we will discuss the basic idea of the theory and note the extent to which empirical information supports it.

A sociological theory of murder

The theory of Henry and Short is based upon the concept, which we discussed earlier, that aggresion is the consequence (although not the sole consequence) of frustration. Thus the relevant social changes are the ones which can result in frustration; of these, Henry and Short are interested primarily in the effect of economic fluctuations on the aggressive behaviors of homicide and suicide. A second important factor in the Henry and Short theory is the Freudian concept that suicide and homicide are opposites—that aggression is either directed inward or directed outward. From this assumption, one would expect that homicide and suicide would increase or decrease differently under different conditions.

Henry and Short suggested that the frustrating effect of economic fluctuation is due to the changes that the fluctuations produce in people's relative social status. One's social position is not an absolute, but can be affected by changes in other people's status. If a man belongs to a low status group, his position is relatively improved when events worsen the situation of the higher status groups. When business improves, on the other hand, the low status person loses relative position because higher status people benefit more than he does and have a greater improvement in status than he can experience. Even if the lower status person's life improves in absolute terms, he is worse off in relative terms. Thus business contraction causes a relative loss in status for the upper classes, and business expansion causes a relative loss in status for the lower classes. Economic depression should thus produce frustration for high status people, while economic improvement should cause frustration for low status people.

Henry and Short assumed, too, that different kinds of people committed homicide and suicide, depending on whether they had learned to direct aggression inward or outward. They felt that lower status groups were more likely to commit murder, while suicide tended to be an upper-class phenomenon. This difference, according to the sociologists, was dependent on child-rearing practices. The method of socialization determined the direction of aggression. The basic, primary target of aggression was assumed to be another person. Either a person would develop into an adult who continued to aggress against others, or he would learn to inhibit his outward aggression and, instead, turn aggression inward onto himself. Only one way of directing aggression is seen as legitimate by a person.

Among people who express aggression outward, there is a tendency toward low superego strength (or conscience) and low experience of guilt feelings. There is evidence that these factors are associated with the experience of physical rather than love-oriented punishment (punishment which deprives the child of the parent's affection and approval) and with punishment by the father rather than by the mother.

Henry and Short then sought to show how experience of love-oriented punishment dealt out by the parent who is the source of nurturance and love leads to the development of tendencies to inhibit the primary other-oriented expression of aggression. This argument centered around the idea that when the source of nurturance and love also administers punishment, then the primary other-oriented expression of aggression threatens to end the flow of love and nurturance. If the child retaliates, he will receive no nurturance. Therefore, he develops habits of inhibiting his primary other-oriented aggression.

One objection to the formulation we have just described is that a correlation between two variables does not necessarily imply a causal consequence. (That is, if all brown-eyed people were right-handed and all blue-eyed people were left-handed, one could not assume that eye color caused hand preference or vice versa.) An alternative explanation of the connection between aggressiveness and punishment experiences is that children who are predisposed by other factors to have low superego strength encourage, or rather facilitate, the use of physical punishment by their parents. Glueck and Glueck (1950) proposed this latter alternative as an explanation of the correlation they found between boys' delinquency and their experience of physical punishment.

Why do some subgroups regard outward-directed aggression as legitimate, while others consider inward-directed aggression to be appropriate? Sociologists have suggested that the strength of external restraints on the group determines this decision. When the demands and expectations of others require rigid conformity, the others become to a great extent responsible for the consequences of behavior. When frustration occurs, then, other people are seen as responsible and thus as targets for the aggression consequent to the frustration. If there are few external restraints, the individual sees himself as responsible for the results of his actions. There is no legitimate reason to turn aggression onto others. In this culture, it is probably the case that low status groups experience the strongest external restraints, in terms of demands of the police, difficulties in keeping a job ("last hired, first fired"), and the lack of financial power over people and circumstances. The upper status groups are much more free to live where they like, go as far in school as they want, work at a chosen career, and break minor laws without risking major punishment. Thus, one would expect lower status groups to legitimize outward-directed aggression, while upper status groups do not.

Empirical tests of the theory

Henry and Short tested empirically some predictions which they derived from their theory. They predicted that *(a)* suicide rates will rise during times of business depression and fall during times of business prosperity, while crimes of violence against people will rise during business prosperity and fall during business depression; and *(b)* the correlation between suicide rates and the business cycle will be higher for high status groups than for low status groups, while the correlation between homicide rates and the business cycle will be higher for low status groups than for high status groups.

Henry and Short felt that their data had confirmed their predictions, but that was not entirely true. They did not have data for many different status categories. The only status category with data available for both homicide and suicide was that of white versus Negro. The correlations between suicide and homicide rates and the business cycle for whites were -.81 and .51, respectively, and for Negroes -.38 and +.49 respectively (Henry and Short, 1954, pp. 29, 49).

In other words, for whites, both suicide and homicide rates went down when the business situation improved, while business contraction was accompanied by a rise in both rates. For blacks, suicide decreased when the economy improved and decreased during business contractions, while homicide rates rose and fell with the economy. Thus, Henry and Short's predictions were true for suicide among whites and for both forms of aggression in blacks, but not for homicide among whites.

The second prediction (point *b* above) was confirmed. The negative correlation between suicide rates and the business cycle was higher for the low status group than for the high status group.

Unfortunately, as Lester (1968) has noted, Henry and Short are occasionally illogical in their deductions about whites and nonwhites of high and low status. For example, during business contraction lower-class whites lose status relative to lower-class blacks. Therefore, they will suffer frustration; their consequent aggression will involve homicide since they are low status people. Thus their homicide rate should increase during business contraction, according to Henry and Short. But their status relative to upper-class whites rises during business contraction, so their frustration and consequent homicide rates should decrease. Which prediction is correct? Is there a rule for deciding which analysis to use? No; in fact the reference groups are deduced after the correlations between suicide and homicide rates and the business cycle have been determined.

Other data support the theory proposed by Henry and Short. For example, Wood (1961) looked at suicide and homicide in the Sinhalese of Ceylon. He found that the suicide rate was lower in those who had no title or property, in those who were unemployed, in those who were unskilled, and in those who spoke no English. He concluded that the suicide rate was lower in those of lower status and lower occupational status. To demonstrate that high status Ceylonese had strong superegos (as Henry and Short's theory demands), he compared completed suicides (who were likely to be of high status) with homicide victims and murderers. He found that the suicides were less likely to be alcoholics, to gamble, to have been convicted of rowdiness, and to have been arrested. He concluded that the higher classes were more strongly committed to the moral code. His data, therefore, do support Henry and Short's thesis since the suicide rate was highest among the members of the better behaved upper classes.

Some evidence which contradicts Henry and Short is found in the work of Lalli and Turner (1968). When these authors looked at the suicide and homicide rates of white and nonwhite males over occupational categories, they found in the United States a general trend for both rates to increase with decreasing social class. This is fine as far as homicide rates go, but the tendency for white suicide rates to rise as social class falls clearly contradicts Henry and Short's expectations.

Gold (1958) concentrated upon one aspect of Henry and Short's theory. He examined the predictions that could be derived if one assumes a relationship between socialization experiences and the expression of aggression. Henry and Short had argued that experience of physical punishment led people to develop habits of expressing aggression outward, whereas experience of psychological punishment led people to express aggression inward. Gold felt that females were more likely to have experienced psychological punishment than were males, Army officers more than enlisted men, whites more than blacks, and urban dwellers more than rural dwellers. Thus females, officers, whites, and urban dwellers should all prefer inward-directed expression of aggression (including suicide) over outward-directed expression of aggression (including homicide) as compared to males, enlisted men, blacks, and rural dwellers respectively.

Gold considered that Henry and Short had been mistaken to use absolute rates of homicide and suicide since the use of absolute rates did not take into account the total number of aggressive acts committed by a societal subgroup. He suggested that a better measure was the suicide rate divided by the combined suicide and homicide rate—in other words, the proportion of suicides among all major aggressive acts. When Gold tested his predictions using this measure of the preponderance of suicide or homicide, his predictions were confirmed for sex, race, urban-rural inhabitance, and army rank.

Gold's suggestion makes good sense. However, Lester (1967) tested the relationship between socialization experiences and the incidence of homicide and suicide in a sample of primitive societies and failed to find the predicted association. The same results occurred whether he used absolute rates or relative rates of suicide and homicide. This failure to confirm Gold's prediction may reflect upon the validity of the postulated relationship between socialization experiences and suicidal behavior, upon the measure suggested by Gold, or upon the methodological inadequacies of Lester's study. (Lester was unable to use a random sample of societies but instead had to use societies for which the required data could be located.)

Littunen and Gaier (1963) tested the ideas of Henry and Short in a study comparing the homicide and suicide rates in Finland and in the United States. They had investigated conformity in the inhabitants of both countries (Gaier and Littunen, 1961) and found that Americans experienced more external restraints than the Finns, in the form of peer group pressures. They therefore predicted that the suicide to homicide ratio would be lower in the United States than in Finland. In 1957 the ratio of the suicide rate to the homicide rate was two in American and ten in Finland, which supported their prediction. Littunen and Gaier would be more convincing, of course, if they had been able to obtain data on conformity in more than just two nations. It would also have been interesting to look at changes in two nations over time. Littunen and Gaier noted the suicide/homicide ratio in the United States and Finland at different times in the twentieth century but they unfortunately had no data on the degree of conformity in the two nations at these different times.

Teele (1965) criticized Henry and Short's notion that other-directed aggression becomes legitimized as the strength of external restraints increases. He felt that the idea was too simple because there are different types of relational systems within which restraints might occur (Teele, 1962). In particular, he noted three systems: familial, religious, and voluntary. Teele suggested that Henry and Short's notion applied to familial and religious relational systems but not to voluntary ones, that is, interaction with friends and participation in voluntary associations. According to Teele, voluntary relational systems lead the individual to be exposed to cultural norms and ethics—ethics which in the case of this culture stress the rights of others. The resulting strong internalization of cultural norms leads the individual to inhibit outward-directed aggression in times of stress and so facilitates suicidal behavior. (These ideas are similar to those of Wood [1961].)

Teele (1962) tried to support his ideas by interviewing psychotic patients who were either assaultive or suicidal. He found that the mothers of the suicidal patients scored significantly higher on a scale of social participation than the mothers of assaultive patients. This result, he concluded, was in accord with his idea since the suicidal patients had been exposed to more people outside the family and thus more of the cultural norms.

Conclusions

The theory of socioeconomic effects on the murder rate presented by Henry and Short is intrinsically interesting and has served to stimulate research. There are some difficulties with it, however, both from the empirical and from the logical points of view. As we have noted, not all research, even that of Henry and Short themselves, has supported the theory. From a theoretical viewpoint, too, there are a number of difficulties present—for instance, the problem of whether to compare the status changes of lower-class whites to upper-class whites or to lower-class blacks. Henry and Short run into difficulty, too, when they attempt to analyze the problem of the murderer who also kills himself.

The latter problem is a particularly good example of the logical difficulties which can crop up when one tries to apply a simple, neat theory to a complex behavior. Henry and Short suggested that murderers who kill primary sources of love and nurturance, like a spouse, will have higher suicide rates than other murderers. But such a prediction is not strictly logical. It may well be that a child whose aggressive act causes him to lose love will learn to direct his aggression inward. An adult, however, should already have developed patterns of handling aggressive impulses prior to marriage, so it is not possible to argue that present loss of nurturance as a result of aggression leads to the development in adulthood of habits of directing aggression against the self.

A further objection can be made about the

problem of the suicidal murderer. Henry and Short set out in their book to show how homicide and suicide are differently determined. Homicide, for example, is characteristic of low status persons, whereas suicide is characteristic of high status persons. Suicide rates and homicide rates are supposed to be differentially affected by the business cycle. But the necessity for dealing with cases in which suicide and homicide are committed by the same person makes nonsense of Henry and Short's whole thesis. If suicide and homicide can be committed by the same person, it is difficult to assert that these behaviors should show different patterns of correlations and associations, especially since the individual's social status is likely to remain relatively constant. If Henry and Short undertook to show how habits either of other-oriented or of self-oriented aggression develop in a person, how could they contemplate both habits occurring in the same individual? Henry and Short suggested that a basically suicidal person projects his internalized or superego demands about behavior onto the victim, thus weakening the internalized prohibition against the outward expression of aggression. This will not do. It enables us to conclude that the basic patterns of aggressive habits which develop according to Henry and Short's analysis are actually of little importance. Secondly, this ploy makes the theory incapable of disproof. Any circumstances can be explained by assuming the existence of projection in one case and denying it in another.

A theory of murder and suicide might better attempt to define the circumstances under which aggression is directed inward or outward by people in different social situations.

Part 5

Cases of murder

Chapter 17

A mass murderer

So-called mass murder, the indiscriminate killing of a large number of people simultaneously, reveals the irrationality of some murderous acts. First, mass murder is especially difficult to conceal or pass off as accidental. It requires special preparations or acts which are public and conspicuous, in which the murderer could scarcely hope to escape notice. Charles Whitman, the Texas Tower killer of some years ago, allowed himself no room for escape and chose a site where his position was easy to detect. Such killers, even more than the ordinary murderer, appear to want to be caught and punished. In addition, most of the victims are strangers to the killer, people against whom he could have had no reasonable, objective grudge. The mass murderer may, like Whitman, simply shoot everyone who comes along, or he may, like the man we will discuss in this chapter, sacrifice the lives of many strangers in order to kill one intimate. This kind of murder can in no sense be considered an attempt at a realistic improvement of life by the removal of some annoying person; instead, it is a totally irrational, emotionally driven, explosion of rage.

The case we are about to examine involved an airplane which crashed eleven minutes after takeoff, killing forty-four people. Two weeks later, a twenty-three-year-old man confessed that he had caused the crash by placing a time bomb in his mother's luggage. He pleaded insanity, but he was found able to stand trial, convicted, and sentenced to execution in the gas chamber, where he died after opposing any appeals.

Before his death, the man, whom we will call Alan, was interviewed by two psychiatrists, Galvin and Macdonald (1959). This chapter will be devoted to a review and discussion of their findings.

Like the other murderers we have discussed, Alan experienced an emotionally cold and disrupted childhood. His parents separated when he was eighteen months old, and he said he had no memory of his father. The mother took Alan and his elder half sister to live with her mother, who cared for the children while the younger woman worked. Alan's mother spent little time with him and made most of her contacts with the children via gifts of toys or money. She was quick-tempered and domineering, often arousing anger in the children, the expression of which she inhibited by presents. Alan reacted to this treatment by developing a number of neurotic traits. He wet his bed, was afraid of being alone, treated animals cruelly, and once set fire to the garage when he was playing with matches.

When the boy's grandmother died, his mother placed him in a home for fatherless boys. There he remained from the age of six to the age of eleven. His adjustment in the home was not good although he stopped wetting the bed as soon as he arrived at the institution. He felt rejected by his mother, and rather realistically so, since she refused to take him out of the institution even after she married a wealthy man when Alan was nine. On several occasions, the boy ran away to his mother, but she sent him back. Finally, when he was eleven, the institution refused to keep him since he had been stealing; they insisted that his mother take care of him.

When Alan was fourteen, he left school to work on his stepfather's ranch. Two years later, assisted by his mother, he lied about his age and joined the Coast Guard. He was discharged six months later after going AWOL. The Coast Guard psychiatric report said:

> This man is an exceedingly immature individual who has exhibited poor judgment and who tends to act on impulses. He is a dependent person, with strong ties to mother. He tolerates frustrations, even those in the normal course of work, very poorly. Other evidences of his poor judgment and impulsive behavior are to be seen in his sleeping on watch, stealing food while on watch, and returning to work drunk. [Galvin and Macdonald, p. 1058]

Alan was flippant about the incident although concerned about the dishonorable discharge. He declared that if he stayed in the Coast Guard and did not get leave, he would go "over the hill" again, in order to see his mother.

In the two years following his discharge from the Coast Guard, Alan held twenty-five different construction and truck driving jobs, scattered all over the United States. He felt that his frequent changes of jobs were due to poor business conditions and the unfair treatment of his bosses.

At nineteen Alan got into his second major conflict with the authorities. He forged over forty checks, amounting to $4,500. With the money, he flew to Seattle and bought a new car, which he used to travel extensively. A few months later, he was arrested after crashing through a roadblock at high speed and was imprisoned for bootlegging and for carrying a concealed weapon. When his real identity was discovered, he was tried for forgery, but he was released on five years' probation, with the stipulation that he repay $1,800 during that period. The rest of the money was repaid by his stepfather.

Two years later came one of the few happy and satisfying episodes of Alan's life. He married a girl whom he had met while studying business administration. His wife seems to have been a warm and accepting person, who provided not only mature satisfactions but also some gratifications of Alan's unsatisfied childhood needs. About his wife, Alan said:

> To me it's the only thing that really matters, it's hard to describe. Some people take their wives for granted. I couldn't. If I came home and she wasn't there I had to find out right away where she was. I wanted to put her away on a shelf and not let anyone else touch her or see her. [Galvin and Macdonald. p. 1059]

There were two children born of the marriage. Following the birth of the second, which was nearly fatal to the wife, Alan was sterlized.

In the second year of Alan's marriage, his mother's influence once again began to intrude strongly into his life. The stepfather died, leaving the mother a large sum of money, which she used to manipulate her son. She insisted on his returning to the university, which he did not want to do. The following year, the mother bought Alan a drive-in movie and went to live with him. The mother had agreed to leave Alan in charge of the drive-in's management, but she insisted upon involving herself in the business affairs. During this time of considerable friction between mother and son, Alan became irritable and short-tempered, but he continued to be dependent on his mother.

The incidents leading up to the bombing of the mother's plane were only revealed some time after the crash. During that period of time, Alan's behavior showed his distress and conflict over what he had done. Even before the plane took off, he could not properly carry out the task of buying insurance policies at the airport. In fact, he accidentally put too many coins in the machine, giving an increased value to the policy on which he was the beneficiary. After the takeoff, having dinner with his family at the airport restaurant, he became nauseated and had to go to the restroom to vomit. When the crash was announced, he cried a great deal, but in the ensuing days made some callous, joking comments about the event. He was soon interviewed by the FBI and confessed to the bombing, but later claimed he had been coerced. While in jail awaiting trial, he made a "suicide attempt" by tightening his socks around his neck. This act and other bizarre behavior led to his hospitalization for observation.

Apparently the strange behavior in jail was intended to simulate insanity. However, Alan behaved reasonably in the hospital, and on the fourth day there again confessed, this time with great emotion, that he had bombed the plane. The event which precipitated the bombing, he said, was his mother's decision to spend Thanksgiving with a relative when he very much wanted her to stay with him. He explained his action this way:

> I tried to tell her how I felt about it. She just said she wouldn't stay, she wouldn't give me any reason at all, no reason why she didn't want to stay. I thought it was the last time she was going to run off and leave me. I wanted to have her to myself for once. Since I was just a little kid she'd leave me with these people, those people. I wanted to get close to her, everytime I'd get close to her she'd just brush me off like I was a piece of furniture, as if I didn't mean more to her than nothing. If she gave me money I was supposed to realize that was enough. I just wanted to do things with her, to sit down and talk to her—just like everybody else's mother would do.
>
> I just had to stop her from going—yet it seemed I had to be free from her, too. She held something over me that I couldn't get from under. When the plane left the ground a load came off my shoulders, I watched her go off for the last time. I felt happier than I ever felt before in my life. I was afraid to do anything without asking her and yet I wanted to go ahead on my own without having to

ask her. Down deep I think she resented me, little things she would do to aggravate me. It's such a relief to tell somebody what I did. It was such a terrible thing I couldn't bear to tell anybody. I deserve to be taken out and shot. I can't find an excuse for something like that. [Galvin and Macdonald, p. 1060]

This impulsive young man had previously used a number of ill-judged attempts at solving problems. He had made four suicide attempts, in addition to the fake attempt in jail. In addition to his previously known criminal record, he confessed to having set fire to a garage when angry because he had been refused a discount on repairs. He showed no evidence of phobias, thought disorders, hallucinations, or delusions, and he was diagnosed as a sociopathic personality—one whose behavior is not much affected by society's more abstract rules.

Even a sociopath does not necessarily murder, of course. In Alan's case, a second factor in his behavior was his intense but ambivalent attachment to his mother. She had always alternated rejecting and indulging him, and the result was a strong dependence on her coupled with powerful hostility and resentment. In spite of all his frustrations, he continued to hope for a really satisfying relationship with her and was made anxious by his negative feelings toward her.

The period of time preceding the bombing increased Alan's tensions in general, as well as those specific to the relationship with his mother. His marriage was good, but the advent of two children in the first two years must have caused some stress on both partners. The drive-in was neither financially successful nor a source of feelings of accomplishment because of the mother's interference. Considering Alan's strong separation anxiety with respect to both his mother and his wife, the near-death of the wife during childbirth must have been unusually distressing. His consequent sterilization, although a practical solution, may have been an additional source of pressure; a young man under the thumb of a "castrating" mother may not benefit emotionally from an act so suggestive of castration. Finally, the continuing stress of his mother's presence, in addition to its simple annoyance value as a source of quarrels, must have constantly reminded him that she did not really care for him as he wanted her to. Perhaps if even one of these sources of stress had been removed, Alan would have been able to resist the impulse to bomb the plane.

Chapter 18

The killer's
private drama

Few murders are committed for grand, impressive reasons. Deep personal hatreds, the desire for revenge, and romantic jealousies are much less often the cause of murder than rage arising from trivial quarrels. This fact suggests that the murderer is actually acting out some private drama, unknown to his victim, rather than killing in order to bring about some desired change in the world. The question must then be: what is the private drama? What event in past or in fantasy is being acted out when a murder is committed? Who are the characters? Whom does the murder victim represent? And who, for that matter, is the murderer? Is he being himself or enacting a parent or a child?

We have made some approaches to these questions in other chapters of this book. In the present chapter, we want to try to show what was happening in the private drama of a single individual, a murderer who was interviewed after his crime was committed (Wilmer, 1969).

Frederick Simpson (a fictitious name) was interviewed when he was twenty-seven years old, shortly before he was paroled from prison. He had served four years of an indeterminate sentence after being convicted of "assault with intent to commit murder," since his victim had been saved by medical care.

Simpson had, at the age of twenty-three, attempted to murder the legal husband of the woman he was living with. Briefly, the murder attempt was as follows. Simpson knocked at the victim's apartment door. He had never seen the victim and asked him to identify himself, which the man did. Simpson then remarked, "I'm going to whip you if you'll step out here. That is if you're man enough." As the man stepped out, Simpson fired a .38 caliber gun three times at close range but hit the victim only twice. The victim fell back into the apartment, pulling closed the door, on which his hand had been resting. Simpson fired two more shots through the door. Ten minutes later, Simpson walked into a police station and handed over his gun, saying that he had just shot a man and that he wanted to go back and finish the job if the victim was not dead.

Simpson's family background was one of confused and unsatisfying relationships with other people. His parents separated when he was seven, and he eventually lived with his mother and stepfather. Both his biological father and his stepfather rejected him. Some of his feelings about the loneliness of his childhood will become apparent when we quote from interviews with him below. One objective piece of evidence about his early difficulties is the record of an arrest when he was fourteen for "bumping against girls in a sexually provocative manner." He was diagnosed at that time as a neurotic child with a transient adolescent maladjustment. He was recommended for psychiatric treatment but never received any.

When Simpson was twenty-two, he married a woman ten years older than himself, who, according to him, was an alcoholic. Unknown to him, she had never been divorced from her previous husband. The wife repeatedly told Simpson of her former husband's mistreatment of her and rejection of her children. Simpson, of course, had no way of knowing whether the wife's allegations were true; he did not even know that she was still legally married.

The attempted murder seems to have been an attempt to settle an issue which existed in a definite form only in Simpson's mind. Wilmer interviewed him in an attempt to find out how the act had come about and what its real meaning was for Simpson. When Simpson was asked about his relationship with his "wife," he said;

> I went to work tending bars ... and I met this woman in there, started living with her, then I married her. ... I think a lot of it was the fact that she had a couple of children ... I've come to the conclusion that the children were the largest attraction. ... She used to tell me stories about

how she had been treated by her ex-husband and I just lapped it up like a puppy dog at a milk tray. . . . She hollered about wanting her kids. I wanted them, too, so one day I just up and drove off to get them. They were in Oklahoma City. So we went back there and got the kids and brought them out. And I tried to be a father to . . . the children. . . . It supplied a need with me. . . . It was a chance to relive my own childhood. [Wilmer, pp. 5-6]

Wilmer, the interviewer, then tried to explore why Simpson was attracted to older women with children. His childhood experience had involved little love or companionship and considerable punishment and rejection. But such circumstances occur in many childhoods, and the result, though never good, is not always an attraction to an older person with children. Simpson's answers to Wilmer suggested that his choice of partners was an attempt to relive his childhood vicariously, to go through the motions of caring for and bringing up the child he had once been. The adult relationship repeated the childhood scene in several respects. In his relationship with his wife's children he tried to have the kind of father-son relationship he had longed for but never had. He tried to replace for them their real father, whom he perceived as equivalent to his rejecting stepfather and his biological father of whom his mother had always complained. The wife completed the picture by complaining about her "ex"-husband in the way that Simpson's mother had complained of hers. Wilmer asked a number of questions about these aspects of the case.

What was your reaction when your wife was telling you these things?

S. Made me angry. Extremely angry.

And?

S. . . . I finally came to the conclusion that this guy was a blot on the face of the earth and the best thing anybody could do was to wipe it off. And that's what I set out to do. . . . He was a threat to me. To the life that I was trying to build. The night this happened, I came home from work and we were sitting there at the table having supper. She tells me she's going to pack the kids and go back to him. Sparked and blew me off . . .

What did you feel like saying?

S. . . . I begged her not to go. . . . She told me that that's what the kids wanted. . . . Eventually she said something about . . . she'd stay there but she'd go over the next day and shoot him . . . That just sort of added fuel to my fire. . . The thought that jumped into mind was . . . This guy is a dirty no good son of a bitch. He deserves to die for what he's done to these people . . . If she goes over there and shoots him, he's dead and she goes to prison. The kids are left with nothing. [Wilmer, pp. 10-12]

Deciding to take his wife's place and commit the murder himself, Simpson took with him both a rifle and a handgun. He had never fired the rifle and did not seem to know why he took both. In fact, he was still doubtful about what to do, as Wilmer's questions revealed.

Did you doubt it?

S. There was doubt, yeah. The biggest thing was

that I always told myself that I could never shoot someone like that. My conscience wouldn't let me. . . . So I was wondering to myself all the way over there. . . . Even when I come up and knock on the guy's door . . . I'm wondering even then, can I do it? The guy opened the door, I said some inane thing to get him to come outside, and I'm still wondering . . . and I was still wondering when the gun went off . . . It was just . . . like the arm was completely divorced from the rest of me. It just blew. I was probably just as much surprised when the gun went off as he was. Because . . . there was no conscious thought of doing it. I was still standing there and my mind wondering whether can I or can't I? [Wilmer, p. 13]

What's going through your mind? Say it out loud.
S. It's kind of blank . . . All the while I wondered, can I do this? Is it physically or mentally possible for me to shoot somebody? Not just necessarily this guy, but anybody. And this was still in my mind . . . I do remember he opened the door and he started to take a step through and Boom! . . . It was a surprise to me too when the gun went off . . . It's like I'm standing here with the gun in my hand but there's another part of me standing back—floating up here watching . . . like it was on film . . . and I'm watching it on a film or something . . . not exactly sure what's going to happen, but powerless to stop anything . . . I was sure that I was aware of what I was doing, but my awareness was off up here on the side someplace, observing . . . The gun went off. The door closed . . . and he—the guy spun. And he had one hand on the

door, when he spun he closed the door. I just fired twice more right through the door. And I don't know why. Except I guess because I could hear the guy holler. And I turned around and I walked off . . . I didn't drive fast. I just walked off. Got in the car and just drove away. I didn't tear out of there 90 miles an hour. I just drove off like normal. . . . I found the phone and called the police department and asked them where's a police station. Told 'em "I just shot guy over here and I'm coming in . . ."

What did you say when you got there?

S. I told them I shot the guy, here's the gun. The sergeant picked it up. I told him to be careful. There's still a couple of bullets in it.

Didn't you think he'd be careful?

S. Well, I—I don't know . . .

What else did you tell the sergeant?

S. Told him it was loaded, still got a couple of rounds in it. He said all right. He just emptied it . . . They asked me to step around here and they started asking me questions. They shook me down and all this . . . and they started booking me . . . I asked them if I was going to be able to make some phone calls and they said, Yeah, when they finished booking me. They took me upstairs and fingerprinted me, photographed me, and all that. Told me to get some sleep. Hour or so later they got me out and took me down and wanted to interview me . . . I was still wound up. They told me . . . the guy's in the hospital, but he might pull through. I told 'em . . . let me go. Let me go finish him. And I was, I was still wound up . . . .

I don't think you believed for a minute that they would take such a statement seriously.
S. Oh no! No! I knew they weren't going to let me go . . . .
Then why did you say it?
S. I don't know. [Wilmer, pp. 15-17]

The interview provides some insight into the private drama which was really being enacted when Simpson tried to kill his paramour's legal husband. As Wilmer noted, the victim, completely unbeknownst to himself, was playing the roles of both Simpson's deserting father and his rejecting stepfather. The common-law wife represented Simpson's mother, and was an appropriate choice for the role because of her greater age. The "stepchildren," in Simpson's thinking, represented himself.

The murder attempt was precipitated when the stepchildren wanted to go back to their real father. This would have been threatening to Simpson in that he did not want to lose the children, but it was especially anxiety-provoking in that it recalled his desire to go back and have a close relationship with his own father.

Simpson's bitter longing for closeness with his father seems to be involved with his decision to take the deer rifle as well as the pistol, a decision which later made no sense to him. One of Simpson's symbols for closeness with his father, a symbol popular in American culture, was the idea of hunting and fishing together. He deeply resented never having been taken fishing by his father. Now, when going to kill the father who never hunted or fished with him, he took a rifle he had bought for deer hunting. (In fact, however, he shot with the handgun only.)

Simpson did not kill his victim although he could easily have done so since he shot at close range. His failure suggests that he was highly ambivalent about his action. On one level, he may have felt that he did not actually want to kill his father, who would then never be able to be close to him. On a more realistic level, he may have recognized that what he was doing was related more to his own feelings than to any events in the objective world. This factor came out when Simpson was interviewed.

> S. After I calmed down and I got to thinking about it . . . This poor son of a bitch . . . Here he got into something he didn't know nothing about. He got hurt . . . that's the thing that's made me feel bad . . . It's the fact that here's a guy who really has not done anything, doesn't know what's happening, and all out of the clear blue sky . . . Boom! Here's somebody shooting at him and he doesn't know really . . . what's going on. [Wilmer, p. 19]

During the course of the murder attempt, Simpson's consciousness of his emotions underwent some interesting changes, many of them indicative of the fact that his act was motivated by deep emotional needs rather than by external reality. He felt angry on his way to the victim's apartment, but once he had confronted him, he felt detached. It was as if he had only been observing at that point, and not feeling. His rage was expressed in the shooting, but he withdrew from the enormity of his act by experiencing no anger, only surprise that his arm suddenly raised a gun and shot the man. (This tendency to repress powerful feelings must have developed in the course of his childhood when even the feeling of anger against his parents would have produced anxiety since he was always so close to losing them completely.) The repression of strong feeling continued until he reached the police station, where, safe among people who would prevent him from committing further violence, he could at last be aware of his turmoil and try to calm down.

The police played an important part in Simpson's emotional drama by assuring him that the world would not allow him to create catastrophe by expressing all the rage that was in him. His rapid trip to the police station after the shooting shows his need for immediate aid in controlling himself, in battling the tendency to "lose his sanity" and go on a rampage of destruction. He even asked the police for a specific verbal statement that they would control him when he asked to be released to go and kill the victim; naturally, as he must have expected, they refused. He was thus reassured that others would maintain the orderliness of the world, which he felt slipping away from him.

Summary

Simpson's case was superficially clear cut in the absence of an analysis of its private meaning. He appeared to be a man simply trying to remove a rival who threatened to take from him his wife and step-children. One might assume that such a man was impulsive, rather stupid, or the product of a violent subculture. Another view might be that he had never been taught to know right from wrong and should be punished until he could make the distinction. An analysis of the event from Simpson's point of view,

The killer's private drama   257

however, shows that there was far more involved than simple rivalry. Had Simpson become involved with a woman who had acted somewhat differently, the stresses of his unsatisfied childhood longings might never have pressed him to attempt to kill. Even if his wife had been involved with another man, Simpson would probably not have attacked the rival had he not had some relationship with the children. This apparently simple case of attempted murder is actually meaningful only when one understands the real needs of the attacker.

Chapter 19

Psychological
evaluation
of a murderer

In the course of the present century, much effort
has gone into the development of tests which will
accurately reveal personality characteristics. Interviews
and records of a person's past life give some information, of course, but such methods are always susceptible
to deliberate misinformation or omission of important
points. The goal of psychological tests has been to
achieve quicker and more incisive techniques of inquiry.
This goal's achievement, we should point out, is still
far in the future. However, psychological test data can
give some important insights into personality.

In this chapter, we will present the psychological
test information derived from the clinical evaluation of
a young male murderer (Wittman and Astrachan, 1949).
This evaluation, as it was originally published, gives little

information about the crime committed (multiple murders were involved), and it does not give the man's
name. However, we have reason to think that the
murderer being tested was the same as one whose
behavior we discussed in another chapter. We will leave
it as a puzzle for the reader to match this murderer's
psychological evaluation with the report of his behavior
given elsewhere.

Appropriate psychological tests

Psychological testing of X focused on several
personality characteristics. There was interest in his
developmental history, with special attention to his
adjustment relative to that of other people of his age.
The developmental history included information on his
progress in school, his physical health, his social
adjustment, his attitudes toward sex and religion. The
Elgin Developmental History, which was used in this
case, also produces a rating of the person's interests as
stressing morality, economic factors, social factors, or
hedonism.

Intelligence testing is also relevant to understanding a murderer's personality. Low intelligence can
add to the stresses the environment places on a potential
killer, and the consequent frustration may make murder
more likely. In addition, since an intelligence test deals
with a number of different abilities, particular strengths
or weaknesses may contribute to the understanding of
personality characteristics. In this case, the test used was
the Wechsler-Bellevue.

The Rorschach test was also used in an attempt to
understand this murderer's ways of thinking and feeling.
This test, of course, is performed by presenting the

subject with symmetrical inkblots and asking him to tell what they look like. Since the blots themselves are ambiguous and represent nothing in particular, responses can only reflect what is going on in the mind of the respondent. Many factors are involved in the interpretation of the results of a Rorschach test; some important ones involve the person's ability to be aware of his feelings, the ways in which he handles sexual or aggressive impulses, and the logicality of his thought processes.

An unusual evaluative method which was used in this case was a "constitutional evaluation"—a personality test based on body type and physical posture. This technique, developed by William Sheldon, uses the idea that personality is largely determined by physical constitution. Body type can lean toward the muscular (personality then being active and emotionally insensitive), the visceral or plump (leading to sociability and hedonism), or the cerebral, thin type (tending toward oversensitivity and difficulty in social situations). Most people combine the three factors to some extent but can be identified as tending toward one component.

In addition to these formal tests, evaluation of X included various questionnaires which tried to get at issues such as his relationship with his family.

Test results

The Elgin Developmental History showed a young man with fair personal adjustment and good adjustment levels relative to school, health, and social interaction. His emotional adjustment and attitudes toward sex were poor. His religious commitment was so extreme that it was also rated as a poor adjustment level. As far as interests and ideals were concerned, there was a stress on morality. The evaluators commented that " . . . his greatest interest was in living as 'good' a life as possible, and concerned with ideas of right and wrong [sic] " (Wittman and Astrachan, p. 88).

How can this be reconciled with the fact that he committed murder? The developmental history suggested that the answer may lie in a state of severe conflict produced by strong precocious sexuality combined with rigid morality. Such a conflict would not necessarily lead to murder in all young men; we will discuss below some other test results which show why X might have made a drastic response to a situation of conflict.

ability was slightly above average. As it happened, X was a college student and had been advanced three grades in elementary and high school. He must thus have been under some stress to maintain his academic standing without a higher intellectual endowment. In addition, X did relatively poorly on tests which require the ability to plan ahead, like arithmetic problems. The evaluators interpreted this difficulty and a problem in sustaining attention as possible evidence of an underlying state of tension. (One source of tension in X's life might have been the pressure of parents who wanted their son to skip a number of grades even though his intelligence was not unusually high.)

Administration of the Rorschach test gave evidence that X was not psychotic. He was in contact with reality and did not suffer from distortions of thinking. X did not seem to be creative or imaginative; he used a concrete approach in solving problems and did not plan ahead or understand interrelationships. His intellectual control was better than his ability to deal with his feelings, so he tended to rationalize about his emotions and to try to inhibit them.

The constitutional evaluation showed that X's body tended toward a combination of muscular and visceral physical traits. He had a great love of physical adventure and a need for vigorous exercise. According to Sheldon's theory, such people tend to have difficulty focusing attention; they are hyperinsulated and tend to miss much that goes on in the world. Sheldon also suggested that people of X's body type have "a relative cleavage, a separate barrier between immediate awareness and the cumulative body of inhibitive, qualifying experience which in most minds lies ready to be re-aroused and associated with the present perception" (quoted by Wittman and Astrachan, pp. 90-91).

In other words, "the individual seems to be cut off horizontally from his own deeper mental levels and resources. . . . When troubled, X's need is for action; the immediate objective is always to get the thing out of his mind, to repress it or dissociate it from focus" (Wittman and Astrachan, p. 91). This tendency would limit X's way of dealing with the sex-religion conflict mentioned above.

The questionnaires given to X got at a number of relevant pieces of information. Among the most important were these: "X has been extremely afraid of something, is bothered by the feeling that things are not real, has many headaches and has frequently felt that someone was hypnotizing him and making him act against his will" (Wittman and Astrachan. p. 89). This fitted in with his statement in an interview that he sometimes felt himself taken over by an alien personality whom he called "G."

Diagnosis

One obvious question about X concerns the presence of psychosis. He had killed a number of people, each act being a violent one. He was obviously not the typical Saturday-night killer who murders in the course of a brawl or quarrel. However, he does not seem to have been consistently psychotic. The murders and some previous robberies were unusual episodes compared to X's ordinary behavior, which was effective and oriented toward reasonable goals. Rarely does a person who can work effectively and who shows good contact with reality also undergo periodic loss of control of this magnitude.

Was X a psychopath? Such a person can commit serious crimes without apparent concern or remorse. He is self-assured and unconcerned with other people's opinion of him. His behavior may be criminal, but it is not usually bizarre or without apparent motive. X does not seem to fit this pattern. He appeared bewildered and confused rather than sure of himself. His crimes had some extremely bizarre elements. In addition, X seemed to show partial amnesia for some of his crimes—a suggestion that guilt and regret were present.

The evaluating clinicians came to the conclusion that X's condition was one of hysteria (a personality disorder characterized by a lack of conscious awareness of conflicts and needs, and by a tendency to forget or be unaware of behavior which satisfies particular needs). Although not psychotic, he was not ordinarily capable of dealing with particular motivations (his precocious sexual development was mentioned above). The conflict between his strict religious training and his other needs was too intense to be resolved in any ordinary way.

When his needs became so strong that they had to be satisfied, the activity occurred in a dissociated state. He identified this state as the period when he was "taken over" by "G." X's usual self-control was absent during the murders, and he was later unable to remember much of what he had done. These reasons were given for concluding that X's condition was an hysterical one:

> There are several points about this case that suggest an hysterical fugue for events when the unacceptable (dissociated) side of X took over. (1) His spontaneous comments that when tensions built up and he was forced out on prowling expeditions, he often did not remember where he went or what he did. Then the next morning he would wake up with a bunch of loot that he didn't remember taking and didn't want. (2) His thermal insensitivity, not feeling cold or hot, regardless of the weather and the way he was dressed. (3) His sudden coming back to full consciousness from an apparent sleep, at times at the scene of his crime, and with only vague and incomplete memory as to how he got there and what he did. (4) His apparent indecision and uncertainty to admit, even to himself, that he had committed murder. On one of these expeditions, he did not remember entering the apartment but when he "awoke" he found a woman dead, a shot fired from his gun, and nobody there who *could* be responsible except himself. Awake, and as himself, X was horrified and frightened at what had been done and in the hope that they would catch this other creature "G." that apparently was a part of him and still

couldn't really be him, he scribbled a note on a mirror, asking that he be caught. (5) When asked specifically if he didn't know that he had killed S and asked how he felt when he read about it in the paper he replied, that he read about it but although he knew he had been out that night he made no attempts to speculate about what had happened. Thus, his attendance at University classes the day after the murder can be explained best not as the cold, unconcern and amorality of a psychopath but as the detachment, "the belle indifference" of a case of hysteria. (6) X's frequent reiterations that he did not know what happened during the murderous attacks and the dismembering of S in the light of his confession would be illogical for one who cooperated as he did with those who interviewed him. He appeared to be anxious to tell everything he knew in the hope that he and others would understand why he behaved as he did. He had no reason to feel that he was making a stronger case for himself by holding any details back, since he had already confessed to the murders and he might *easily* have felt that he would antagonize and alienate the examiners by withholding details. [Wittman and Astrachan, p. 93]

The case of X, of course, is not that of a typical murderer. We must repeat once again that the usual murder is an act of anger occurring during some trivial quarrel. The kind of killing X committed, however, is among the most frightening of all murders because it is unpredictable, the victim is an innocent stranger, and the act is likely to be repeated. Psychological evaluation of such killers is important because the information it gives may help to identify and treat other potential "motiveless" murderers.

However, as the reader may have concluded, the psychological tests which are presently available are in no sense "litmus paper" which can be trusted to detect homicidal tendencies. Certainly, no single test is an accurate predictor of murder. The contribution of psychological testing to the study of murder will probably lie in the identification of complex patterns of results on many different tests.

Part 6

Conclusions about murder

Chapter 20

Preventing murder

Human beings have for thousands of years concerned themselves with the punishment to be meted out
to murderers. Only in the last hundred years or so have
they as seriously tried to understand what causes
murder. A concern with the prevention of murder is
more recent still. Where such a concern does exist
today, it is most frequently directed toward the
prevention of recidivism in jailed murderers, rather than
the prevention of any murder in the first place.

A public health approach has proved useful in the
eradication of such problems as smallpox and cholera. It
may be the case, too, that it can help in the prevention
of murder. Hankoff (1966) has suggested using the
public health approach, dividing homicide prevention
into primary, secondary, and tertiary levels. The present

271

chapter will be devoted to examining how one might apply this approach to homicide prevention.

Levels of prevention

1. The tertiary level of prevention is the attempt to prevent further serious aggression by those who have already committed violent acts. Hankoff suggested that this is a long-term task, that a murderer should be considered a permanent public charge who would be under lifelong psychiatric care. The psychiatric treatment might be given in prison or through the cooperation of a psychiatrist and a probation officer.

As the reader can imagine, the cost to the public of providing long-term expert psychiatric care for the 9,000 murderers this country produces each year would be rather high. Hankoff's suggestion might be more practical if treatment were concentrated on groups for whom a repeat murder is unusually likely. On the whole, recidivism among murderers is low (0.5 percent over twenty years, according to Macdonald, 1967). However, there are some groups for whom a subsequent murder is relatively probable. Baker (1959), for example, reported two repeat murders, soon after release from prison, out of eight convicted American Indian murderers.

2. The secondary level of prevention deals with people who have not yet murdered but who are on the verge of doing so. Working at this level of prevention involves early detection of the homicidal person, which Hankoff felt was impossible with the present state of knowledge. Generally, the only likely time for such detection is in a situation in which the homicidal person turns to a counseling or mental health facility.

A crucial role in "homicide detection" can be played by these services, especially by the twenty-four-hour telephone crisis counseling services now found in most major cities since some homicidal people do call for help at times when they are frightened by their impulses. The telephone service, if properly advertised, could perform an important service in dealing with the potential murderer since he will find its resources available at all times of night and day. The informality and ease of contact present in telephone counseling could be crucial in helping a person deal with impulses which will not wait until a counseling center opens the following morning.

A second resource for early homicide detection lies in the so-called "gatekeeper" programs presently being initiated in cities. These programs organize community workers including the police, clergymen, and physicians, and others who come into contact with the public, such as bartenders and prostitutes (the latter groups seem particularly effective when trained). Gatekeepers have as their primary function detection, screening, and referral to professional workers, but they are also good at intervening therapeutically when an appropriate conversation gets started. The gatekeeper program formalizes the helping functions of people like bartenders, whom many people perceive as sympathetic ears. It also provides an extra dimension in their help by enabling the gatekeepers to refer "patients" to more highly trained therapists when the need exists.

3. Primary prevention seeks to prevent violent tendencies from developing in a society or an individual. It is thus the most difficult level to work at, both theoretically and practically.

The difficulty of primary prevention

One of the thorniest problems for primary prevention of murder has to do with the apparent critical importance of childhood experiences. Of all areas of behavior, the method of child rearing chosen by parents is probably the touchiest. Parents do not like to be told how to deal with their children; this is particularly true of the parents whose children are likely to grow up murderers. A long tradition declares children to be their parents' chattels, in whose welfare the community may take an interest only if there is the most gross parental neglect. In addition, parents usually like their children to be like themselves. If the parents are habitually violent, or, alternatively, if they are unable to express aggression appropriately, these traits are the ones they will enjoy seeing in their children. They will not want to see their children grow up "outsiders" to the family, no matter how much the community prefers the kind of person who is unlike the family under consideration.

Whatever the practical problems involved in primary homicide prevention, undoubtedly the most effective prevention would result from teaching all children how to use acceptable outlets for aggression. Most ideas about primary prevention have taken the related tack of removing stimulation which might teach children to use unacceptable means of aggression. For instance, the mass media are under pressure to cut down the number of scenes of violence they present because of the possibility that children will copy the undesirable behavior. Similarly, recent years have seen a revulsion against the use of war toys for children, and toy companies have reacted to pressure by converting toys like "G. I. Joe" into less overtly aggressive objects.

There have unfortunately been fewer suggestions about how to encourage the development of acceptable habits of expressing anger. Hankoff suggested that one way of doing this would be the creation of outlets like paramilitary organizations for lower-class youths. In such organizations boys could learn the control over overt aggression which is absent in their homes, while simultaneously maintaining a positive (because apparently aggressive) self-image. The street gang may in fact act as an informal organization of this nature because it teaches and requires some control; although members of rival gangs may be fought and killed, such aggression can take place only under particular circumstances, and members of one's own gang are not on the whole a target of aggression.

For another suggestion, we have turned to a utopian novel. Aldous Huxley (1962), in *Island*, described an educational system in which children are taught to express rage without doing harm to others. In one scene, school children are being taught about "redirecting the power generated by bad feelings" by learning to dance the Rakshasi Hornpipe.

> "So stamp it out," the children were shouting in unison. And they stamped their small sandaled feet with all their might. "So stamp it out!" A final furious stamp and they were off again, jigging and turning, into another movement of the dance. . . .
> "A Rakshasi [one of the characters explains] is a species of demon. Very large, and exceedingly unpleasant. All the ugliest passions personified. The Rakshasi Hornpipe is a device for letting off those dangerous heads of steam raised by anger and frustration." [P. 228]

Such deliberate instruction on the appropriate channeling of aggression is rare in everyday life. Some parents teach a temporary inhibition of rage by counseling the child to "count to ten" or "take five deep breaths" before expressing anger. Others may encourage the young child to use a "tantrum corner" in which he can express anger without hurting himself or inviting retaliation from others. On the whole, though, most parental teaching about aggression is a confusing mixture of "Don't you dare look at me that way" and "Didn't you hit him back? Are you some kind of sissy?" The reason for the confusion probably lies in the parent's own conflicts about aggression. He believes simultaneously that anger should be controlled and that the person who loses fights is unworthy of respect. As long as such mixed attitudes remain, it is not likely that parents can teach healthy and appropriate ways of expressing rage.

Secondary prevention: recognizing the potential killer

Identifying the potential murderer is not an easy task. One knows that he is likely to be a young male and that nonwhites have a higher homicide rate than whites. It is also known that murders take place more commonly on weekends and that the murderer and the victim have frequently been drinking (Wolfgang, 1958). Patients with diagnoses of schizophrenia, especially if there is paranoid ideation, are suspect. If the patient has threatened to kill someone, the risk that he will kill is greater. If the patient has a record of assault (or of previous murder), then the risk of subsequent murder is greater. If the patient has the means to murder and has formulated a plan, the likelihood of killing is greater.

Macdonald (1967) noted that the absence of previous suicide attempts in those threatening homicide suggests an increased risk of subsequent homicide. Recent stresses and lack of resources contribute to the risk. Macdonald also noted that provocative behavior by potential victims should be a clue considered in evaluating the risk of murder.

Perhaps worth emphasizing is the point that in many cases the murderer continually threatened his relatives prior to the actual killing. In many cases, the relatives, friends, and even the police were reluctant to charge the person or refer him to psychiatric care. An educational program should be designed to help the public realize the danger from violent and threatening individuals and to encourage them to seek professional help. These professionals must in turn be educated to respond to such requests for help.

Resnick (1969), after reviewing research into infanticide, noted that about three-quarters of the parents who murdered their own children had shown signs of psychiatric disturbance prior to the murder. Some mothers had talked openly of suicide and expressed concern for their children's future. Some 40 percent of the murdering parents were seen by a physician or psychiatrist shortly before the crime. Thus, there is often an opportunity to detect the impending crisis and prevent the murder. Resnick suggested that physicians should be alert to the possibility of infanticide in distressed parents. He argued for access to immediate psychiatric care, prompt intervention in cases of child abuse (which often turn into infanticide by accident), and the need for social agencies to be cognizant of the need for taking unwanted children.

Malmquist (1971), after studying twenty adolescent murderers, described some prodromal cues—symptoms which suggest that a person is likely to kill soon.

1. Behavioral changes within forty-eight hours before the murder include mood shifts, cognitive changes, pessimism, and self-critical brooding.

2. Calls for help attempt to communicate the potential murderer's building crisis of rage, but are usually not noticed or denied by friends and relatives.

3. An increase in the use of barbiturates and tranquilizers is common. The potential murderer is often on amphetamines.

4. Losses of loved ones, jobs, and so on make the crisis situation more serious.

5. Threats to manhood—scorn or criticism by a spouse or lover, failure at an important task, for example—add to the likelihood of murder.

6. The growing murderous crisis is reflected in physical problems. There may be genuine recurring medical difficulties, or somatization of emotions (e.g., a constantly upset stomach), or hypochondriacal preoccupations.

7. The occurrence of homosexual advances from others adds to the potential murderer's difficulties.

8. A final, and very important, sign is the development of an emotional crescendo leading up to the murder. This includes a build-up of agitation and energy, motor restlessness, disturbances in sleeping and eating, restless pacing and muttering, crying and sobbing spells, and panicky states of acute anxiety.

Some of these cues, of course, can occur in nonmurderous emotional states or even in the course of normal life. But each of them, when taken together with other cues, indicates something about the seriousness of the possibility of murder. The more of the cues that are present, the more likely murder becomes. The two cues that are most helpful in diagnosing the imminence of murder are the first and the last: behavioral changes and the development of an emotional crescendo.

As we mentioned in earlier chapters, some murderers may be described as overcontrolled in their expression of aggression, while others are undercontrolled. The *undercontrolled* murderer has poor inhibitions against aggression and responds aggressively to all frustration. His control over aggression is not completely lacking. He exercises control over the kind and extent of aggression he commits. For example, when he murders, he tends not to be brutal or sadistic. If there are restrictions against showing aggression toward certain people, then he is able to displace his aggression onto other people. However, he cannot inhibit his aggressive responses as easily as most people, and he is constantly involved in violent scrapes. He is often diagnosed as a sociopathic personality because of his pattern of behavior.

In contrast to the undercontrolled murderer, the *overcontrolled* killer has abnormally rigid controls against aggressing. No matter what the provocation, he rarely responds angrily. His inhibitions are so great that he often cannot release aggression by displacing it or substituting a less drastic act. Since he is unable to obtain the slightest release for his anger, it builds up until it is so great that his inhibitions fail to control it. A minor frustration can then bring about some catastrophic, completely inappropriate act of aggression. After this explosive event, he often returns to his former unaggressive state.

The existence of these two distinct types of murderers suggests that a single rating or diagnostic scale may not be adequate for prediction of a murder. The prodromal cues for murder may be different in the undercontrolled and the overcontrolled murderers, whose general ways of behaving differ considerably.

Secondary prevention: management
of the homicidal person

[A second problem of secondary homicide prevention involves the management of the homicidal person after he is identified. There is far less literature on the management of the person with homicidal impulses than on the care of the potential suicide.] However, it is not uncommon for patients in therapy to have feelings of hatred directed toward others. [Occasionally, the person may threaten homicide and have the means to carry out murder.] What can the therapist do in such a case?

Kuehn and Burton (1969) reported the cases of three students who went to a college counseling service because of their desire to commit murder. Several suggestions for management were offered.

1. *Recognition:* To recognize the homicidal patient, intense, directive questioning is needed. In particular, the counselor should focus upon intense hostile thoughts, the capacity to carry out threats, and the presence of preliminary actions which would tend to lead to the performance of the homicidal act. The counselor must not shirk asking these questions.

2. *Consultation:* Homicidal patients arouse much anxiety in counselors. Kuehn and Burton suggested that staff seek consultation in cases where the patient is homicidal and that conjoint interviews be conducted. The patients should not be left alone in the center and telephone calls should be made in their presence so that they can see and hear what is going on. Since homicidal patients tend to be paranoid, this lack of secrecy prevents the paranoid ideation from feeding on the counselor's behavior. If responsibility for management of the patient is shared, then individual staff anxiety is reduced.

3. *Hospitalization:* If the homicidal threats are judged to be serious and if there is a good chance that the patient may kill someone, then hospitalization is called for. This will arouse paranoid ideation in the patient, quite realistically. Kuehn and Burton recommended hospitalization in a general medical center rather than in a psychiatric hospital in order to decrease the patient's fears. The patient may be helped to deal with his fears by the encouragement of intellectualization and rationalization, by interpreting his fears about hurting others and about what might happen to him as a result of admitting his homicidal tendencies, and by urging his *voluntary* hospitalization.

Involuntary hospitalization is difficult to carry out in these cases, unless the patient is grossly disturbed, since our ability to predict who will murder is limited. However, in extreme cases a temporary restraining order can be obtained if someone is prepared to lodge a complaint.

4. *Other treatment:* Kuehn and Burton urged that the patient receive adequate psychotherapy and oral doses

of tranquilizers. It seems to help if the physician remains with the patient while the medication takes effect and even helps him into bed. Adequate follow-up is crucial after the patient is through the homicidal crisis. Kuehn and Burton noted that, after a few days in the hospital, the patient's anxiety decreases, and pre-psychotic defenses become strengthened. The patient soon becomes able to consider alternatives to his present mode of living. An important aspect of the treatment is to encourage the patient to view the clinic as a place to seek help, so that he will use it again if there is another homicidal crisis.

Secondary prevention: the deterrent concept

A time-honored consideration in the secondary prevention of homicide is the notion that severe punishment of the murderer has a deterrent effect on others who might kill. This argument is raised every time a state or nation proposes to abolish the death penalty for murder. In fact, however, there is little evidence that the existence of severe punishment acts in any way to cut down the murder rate or that abolition of such punishment leads to an increase in murder.

Tertiary prevention: preventing repeat murders

For most social or physical disturbances, the prevention of recurrence is of considerable concern. In the case of homicide, though, there is little problem of recidivism. Murderers do not usually kill again. The rate of repeated murder is only 0.5 percent over twenty years following the first killing. This is true in spite of the fact that most murderers are in prison for a relatively short period of time (and it should be remembered, too, that there are plenty of opportunities to kill while in jail).

Some final remarks

Legislation to regulate the availability of guns has been suggested as a way to prevent homicide. It is notable that similar measures are occasionally proposed for the prevention of suicide, but they are not successful in achieving that end. Detoxification of gas in Switzerland and restriction of sales of parathion in Finland did not appear to reduce the suicide rate, but they did affect the methods chosen for suicide. (Lester, 1972). One might expect a similar effect on homicide—change in methods, but no reduction in the rate.

However, Tanay (1972) suggested that the availability of weapons might make a difference to some kinds of murderers. He categorized murderers into two kinds. *Ego-syntonic* murderers are those who act without disruption in the functioning of the ego and who find the murder consciously acceptable. The ego-syntonic murder is a rational, goal-directed act, and fulfills a conscious wish. Tanay suggested that punitive measures might be an effective deterrent for this kind of murder.

Ego-dystonic murders are killings that occur against the conscious wishes of the murderer. Usually the conscious state of the killer is changed—a dissociative state. The ego-dystonic murderer resembles the overcontrolled murderer described above, and his murders are usually explosively violent. Tanay felt that punitive measures are useless as deterrents for such murderers but that availability of weapons may be relevant to their acts. He felt that restriction of guns in particular might reduce the incidence of this kind of homicide. The trouble with this suggestion is that murder is easily carried out by knife, blunt instrument, cord, or hands; restriction of these particular methods is hardly a feasible proposal.

Chapter 21

The making
of murderers

As an exercise for people studying suicide, Norman Farberow once posed the question: how would one bring up a child so that he would be likely to kill himself? This question, although superficially a callous one, is actually a useful approach to many problems of undesirable behavior. Knowing how to create a suicide or a murderer or an exhibitionist does not necessarily specify exactly how to avoid the development of people with such problems, but it offers an excellent start. For this reason we here describe the most likely background for murderers of two different types.

The most important factors in the developmental history of a murderer are probably these: (1) attitudes of mother; (2) attitudes of father; (3) consistency and length of close association with either or both parents;

(4) physical damage at birth or later; (5) experience of physical abuse; (6) observation of physical struggles and quarreling; and (7) rigidity of training about impulse control.

Considering these seven factors, this might be the way to produce the sort of person who quarrels with a friend in a tavern, draws the gun he always carries on Saturday nights, and murders:

A boy would be born prematurely to poorly educated parents while his mother was still in her teens, and he would be followed rapidly by six siblings. During his early childhood, the boy would witness many family disputes. The father would often be absent because of anger or job necessities. The family's income would be sporadic because of the father's irregular employment. The father's temper would often be short, and he occasionally would impose severe and unexpected discipline upon the children—especially on his oldest son, who his father would insist must be forced to "be a man."

The mother would be less deliberately severe, but her fatigue and anger at the demands of her brood would lead her to be careless; thus the boy would experience a number of fairly severe accidents while still quite young. A complicating factor in the household would be the mother's elder brother, who would single out the boy for unpleasant practical jokes and frightening approaches made "in fun." These attacks would be tacitly approved by the mother, who would also call upon her brother to discipline the boy when his father was absent. The uncle would most often be asked to spank the boy for bedwetting. The effect of the boy's association with his uncle would reach a peak when he was five and his mother had to spend eighteen months in a tuberculosis sanitarium.

The boy would experience little success in school, but he would manage to get along until high school when his late adolescence would isolate him from his coevals, resulting in much troublemaking calculated to win attention and prove his "manliness." Eventually the boy's misbehavior in school would lead to his dropping out and joining the army. There, he would win approval by becoming an expert marksman, but he would frequently be in trouble for his truculent attitude toward officers. Eventually he would be given a general discharge following a brawl in which a companion was severely injured.

The boy would not yet be nineteen when he found himself discharged, with little education and few skills. It would be only a matter of time before his irritability and skill with a gun combined with his anger over frustrations and produced an impulsive murder.

What might be the background of a murderer who suddenly and brutally kills a woman with whom he is said to have had a Platonic relationship? The same seven factors are again essential, but the pattern is considerably different:

This boy would be the only child born to middle-aged parents who had married late. The mother, a former kindergarten teacher with strict ideas on the rearing of children, would refuse intercourse after the boy's birth. The father, a mild-mannered, withdrawn person, would accept this as he did his wife's other whims. He would live essentially as a boarder in their home and take little part in his son's care and education. The mother would have as her goal the rearing of a "perfect child"—obedient, quiet, and happy to play by himself or do little jobs to help his mother. She would be especially concerned that her son develop no "bad habits" such as interest in sex or displays of anger and aggressiveness.

The boy would be a bright child and a quick learner, and he would thus internalize his mother's lessons to such an extent that he could not voluntarily disobey them. At the same time, he would get so much praise and approval from his mother (at least during his school years) that the relationship would be highly rewarding as well as frustrating in its demands for repression of basic motivations.

Some of the satisfactions of the tie between mother and son would disappear as he moved into his high school and college years. Gradually it would become clear that he was missing all chances for contact with the opposite sex. By the time he graduated from college, he would be far behind other men of his age in the social skills needed to develop heterosexual relationships. By this point it would scarcely matter whether or not the mother was still living; the rigid restraints she had taught, resulting in the inherent frustrations of a life lacking any expression of anger or sexuality, would continue until one too many broke down the restraints, and a violent murder of another woman would occur.

Neither of these men's early lives involved serious neglect or maltreatment. But patterns of apparently minor childhood experiences like theirs are the roots of murder.

References

Abrahamsen, D. A study of Lee Harvey Oswald. *Bulletin of the New York Academy of Medicine,* 1967, 43, 861-888.

Ansbacher, H. L., Ansbacher, R., Shiverick, D., & Shiverick, K. Lee Harvey Oswald. *Psychoanalytic Review*, 1966, 53, 55-68.

Ardrey, R. *African genesis.* New York: Atheneum, 1961.

Baker, J. L. Indians, alcohol, and homicide. *Journal of Social Therapy,* 1959, 5, 270-275.

Banay, R. S. Study in murder. *Annals of the American Academy of Political Science,* 1952, 284, 26-34.

Barrett, G. W., & Franke, R. H. "Psychogenic" death. *Science,* 1970, 167, 304-306.

Batt, J. C. Homicidal incidence in the depressive psychoses. *Journal of Mental Science,* 1948, **94,** 782-793.

Bedau, H. A. (Ed.) *The death penalty in America.* Garden City, N.Y.: Doubleday, 1967.

Bender, L. Children and adolescents who have killed. *American Journal of Psychiatry,* 1959, **116,** 510-513.

Bender, L., & Curran, F. J. Children and adolescents who kill. *Journal of Criminal Psychopatholgy,* 1940, **1,** 297-322.

Berg, I. A., & Fox, V. Factors in homicides committed by 200 males. *Journal of Social Psychology,* 1947, **26,** 109-119.

Bettelheim, B. *The informed heart.* Glencoe, Ill.: Free Press, 1960.

Blackburn, R. Personality in relation to extreme aggression in psychiatric offenders. *British Journal of Psychiatry,* 1968a, **114,** 821-828.

———. Emotionality, extraversion, and aggression in paranoid and nonparanoid schizophrenic offenders. *British Journal of Psychiatry,* 1968b, **114,** 1301-1302.

Blackman, N., Weiss, J. M. A., & Lamberti, J. W. The sudden murderer. *Archives of General Psychiatry,* 1963, **8,** 284-294.

Blumenthal, M. D. Predicting attitudes toward violence. *Science,* 1972, **176,** 1296-1303.

Bohannon, P. *African homicide and suicide.* Princeton: Princeton University Press, 1960.

Bonkalo, A. Electroencephalography in criminology. *Canadian Psychiatric Association Journal,* 1967, **12,** 282-286.

Burton-Bradley, B. G. The amok syndrome in Papua and New Guinea. *Medical Journal of Australia,* 1968, 1, 252-256.

Buss, A. H. *The psychology of aggression.* New York: Wiley, 1961.

Cerbus, G. Seasonal variation in some mental health statistics. *Journal of Clinical Psychology,* 1970, 26, 61-63.

Chrzanowski, R. & Szymusik, A. Results of pneumo-encephalography in a group of murderers, *Polish Medical Journal,* 1970, 9, 758-764.

Cole, K. E., Fisher, G., & Cole, S. S. Women who kill. *Archives of General Psychiatry,* 1968, 19, 31-38.

Cormier, B. M. On the history of men and genocide. *Canadian Medical Association Journal,* 1966, 94, 276-291.

Cruvant, B. A., & Waldrop, F. N. The murderer in the mental institution. *Annals of the American Academy of Political Science,* 1952, 284, 35-44.

Davidson, G. M. Psychiatric aspects of the law and of homicide. *Psychiatric Quarterly Supplement,* 1946, 20, 30-49.

Despert, J. L. *The emotionally disturbed child.* New York: Doubleday, 1965.

Dollard, J., Doob, L., Miller, N., Mowrer, O., & Sears, R. *Frustration and aggression.* New Haven: Yale University press, 1939.

Dorpat, T. L. Suicide in murderers. *Psychiatric Digest,* 1966, 27 (June), 51-55.

——·Psychiatric observations on assassinations. *Northwest Medicine,* 1968, 67, 976-979.

Ervin, F. The biology of individual violence. In D. Mulvihill, M. Tumin, & L. Curtis (Eds.), *Crimes of violence, volume 13.* Washington, D.C.: United States Government Printing Office, 1969. Pp. 1017-1037.

Ewing, J. F. Juramentado. *Anthropological Quarterly,* 1955, **28,** 148.

Eysenck, H. J. *Crime and personality.* Boston: Houghton-Mifflin, 1964.

Farberow, N. L., & Shneidman, E. S. (Eds.) *The cry for help.* New York: McGraw-Hill, 1961.

Fenton, G. W., Tennent, T. G., Cornish, K.A., & Rattray, N. The EEG and sex chromosome abnormalities. *British Journal of Psychiatry,* 1971, **119,** 185-190.

Freedman, L. Z. Assassination. *Postgraduate Medicine,* 1965, **37,** 650-658.

Freeman, M. A social and ecological analysis of the systematic female infanticide among the Nestilik Eskimo. *American Anthropologist,* 1971, **73,** 1011-1018.

Friedrich, P. Assumptions underlying Tarascan political homicide. *Psychiatry,*1962, **25,** 315-327.

Gaier, E. L., & Litunen, Y. Modes of conformity in two subcultures. *Acta Sociologica,* 1961, **5,** 65-75.

Galvin, J. A. V., & Macdonald, J. M. Psychiatric study of a mass murderer. *American Journal of Psychiatry,* 1959, **115,** 1057-1061.

Garfinkel, H. Research notes on inter- and intra-racial homicides. *Social Forces,* 1949, **27,** 369-381.

Gibbens, T. C. N. Sane and insane homicide. *Journal of Criminal Law and Criminology,*1958, **49,** 110-115.

Gibbs, J., & Martin, W. *Status integration and suicide.* Eugene: University of Oregon Press, 1964.

Glaser, D., Kenefick, D., & O'Leary, V. *The violent*

offender. Washington, D.C.: United States Government Printing Office, 1968.

Glueck, S., & Glueck, E. *Unraveling juvenile delinquency.* New York: Commonwealth Fund, 1950.

Gold, M. Suicide, homicide, and the socialization of aggression. *American Journal of Sociology,* 1958, 63, 651-661.

Guttmacher, M. *The mind of the murderer.* New York: Farrar Strauss, 1960.

Halbwachs, M. *The causes of suicide.* Paris. Felix Alcan, 1930.

Hankoff, L. D. Psychiatric and public health aspects of the prevention and treatment of violence. *Journal of the Hillside Hospital,* 1966, 15, 94-103.

Hastings, D. W. The psychiatry of presidential assassinations. *Journal-Lancet,* 1965 85, 93-100, 157-162, 189-192, 294-301.

Hendin, H. *Black suicide.* New York: Basic Books, 1969.

Henry, A., & Short, J. *Suicide and homicide.* Glencoe, Ill.: Free Press, 1954.

Huxley, A. *Island.* New York: Harper & Row, 1962.

Jackson, D. The evoluation of an assassin. *Life,* 1964, Time Inc., February 21, 68-80.

Jesse, F. T. *Murder and its motives.* London: Harrar, 1952.

Kahn, M. W. A comparison of personality, intelligence, and social history of two criminal groups. *Journal of Social Psychology,* 1959, 49 33-40.

——. Superior performance IQ of murderers as a function of overt act or diagnosis. *Journal of Social Psychology,* 1968, 76, 113-116.

Katz, J. On the death of the president. *Psychoanalytic Review,* 1965, **51**, 661-664.

Kuehn, J. L., & Burton, J. Management of the college student with homicidal impulses. *American Journal of Psychiatry,* 1969, **125**, 1594-1599.

Kurland, A., Morgenstern, J., & Sheets, C. A comparative study of wife murderers admitted to a state psychiatric hospital. *Journal of Social Therapy,* 1955, **1**(2), 7-15.

Lalli, M., & Turner, S. Suicide and homicide. *Journal of Criminal Law, Criminology, and Police Science,* 1968, **59**, 191-200.

Langberg, R. Homicide in the United States. *Vital Health Statistics,* 1967, series 20, 1-33.

Lester, D. Suicide, homicide, and the effects of socialization. *Journal of Personality and Social Psychology,* 1967, **5** 466-468.

——. Henry and Short on suicide. *Journal of Psychology* 1968, **70** 179-186.

——. Suicide and homicide. *Social Psychiatry,* 1971, **6,** 80-82.

——. *Why people kill themselves.* Springfield: Thomas, 1972.

——. Variation in homicide rate with latitude and longitude in the United States. *Perceptual and Motor Skills,* 1973, **36**, 532.

Lester, G., & Lester, D. *Suicide.* Englewood Cliffs, N.J.: Prentice-Hall, 1971.

Lindner, R. *The fifty minute hour.* New York: Holt, Rinehart & Winston, 1954.

Littunen, Y., & Gaier, E. L. Social control and social integration. *International Journal of Social Psychiatry,* 1963, **9**, 165-173.

Lorenz, K. *On aggression.* New York: Harcourt Brace Jovanovich, 1966.

Macdonald, J. M. The threat to kill. *American Journal of Psychiatry*

——. Homicidal threats, *American Journal of Psychiatry*

Malmquist, C. Premonitory signs of homicidal aggression in juveniles. *American Journal of Psychiatry*, 1971, 128, 461-465.

Marshall, J. *Law and psychology in conflict.* Garden City, N.Y.: Doubleday, 1969.

Matthew, J. R., & Constan, E. Six and fourteen dysrhythmia and the ego. *Journal of Neuropsychiatry*, 1964, 5, 490-494.

McClearn, G. E. Biological bases of social behavior with special reference to violent behavior. In D. Mulvihill, M. Tumin, & L. Curtis (Eds.), *Crimes of violence, volume 13.* Washington, D.C.: United States Government Printing Office, 1969. Pp. 979-1010.

Meerloo, J. A. M. *Suicide and mass suicide.* New York: Grune & Stratton, 1962.

Megargee, E. I. Assault with intent to kill. *Trans-Action*, 1965, 2(6), 27-31.

——. Undercontrolled and overcontrolled personality types in extreme antisocial aggression. *Psychological Monographs*, 1966, 80, #, whole no. 611.

——. A critical review of theories of violence. In D. Mulvihill, M. Tumin, & L. Curtis (Eds.), *Crimes of violence, volume 13.* Washington, D.C.: United States Government Printing Office, 1969. Pp. 1037-1115.

Megargee, E. I., & Mendelsohn, G. A. A cross-validation

of twelve MMPI indices of hostility and control. *Journal of Abnormal and Social Psychology,* 1962, **65,** 431-438.

Menninger, K., & Mayman, M. Episodic dyscontrol. *Bulletin of the Menninger Clinic,* 1956, **20,** 153-165.

Michaels, J. J. Enuresis in murderous aggressive children and adolescents. *Archives of General Psychiatry,* 1961, **5,** 490-493.

Mowrer, O. H. *Learning theory and the symbolic process.* New York: Wiley, 1960.

Munsterberg, H. *On the witness stand.* New York: Boardman, 1923.

Ogden, M., Spector, M., & Hill, C. Suicide and homicides among Indians. *Public Health Reports,* 1970, **85,** 75-80.

Owen, D. The 47, XYY male. *Psychological Bulletin,* 1972, **78,** 209-233.

Palmer, S. *A study of murder.* New York: Crowell, 1960.

——. Murder and suicide in 40 nonliterate societies. *Journal of Criminal Law, Criminology, and Police Science,* 1965, **56,** 320-324.

Parker, S. The Wiitiko psychosis in the context of Ojibwa personality and culture. *American Anthropologist,* 1960, **62,** 603-623.

Pettigrew, T. F., & Spier, R. E. Ecological structure and Negro homicide. *American Journal of Sociology,* 1962, **67,** 621-629.

Pokorny, A. D. Moon phases, suicide, and homicide. *American Journal of Psychiatry,* 1964, **121,** 66-67.

——. Human violence. *Journal of Criminal Law, Criminology, and Police Science,* 1965, **56,** 488-497.

——. A comparison of homicide in two cities. *Journal*

of Criminal Law, Criminology, and Police Science, 1965, **56**, 479-487.

——. Sunspots, suicide, and homicide. *Diseases of the Nervous System*, 1966, **27**, 347-348.

Pokorny, A. D., & Davis, F. Homicide and the weather. *American Journal of Psychiatry*, 1964, **120**, 806-808.

Pokorny, A. D., & Mefferd, R. B. Geomagnetic fluctuations and disturbed behavior. *Journal of Nervous and Mental Disease*, 1966, **143**, 140-151.

Porterfield, A. L. Indices of suicide and homicide by states and cities. *American Sociological Review*, 1949, **14**, 481-490.

——. Suicide and crime in folk and secular society. *American Journal of Sociology*, 1952, **57**, 331-338.

——. Ecological correlates of alcoholism. *Social Problems*, 1958, **5**, 326-338.

Progoff, I. The psychology of Lee Harvey Oswald. *Journal of Individual Psychology*, 1967, **23**, 37-47.

Quinney, R. Suicide, homicide, and economic development. *Social Forces*, 1965, **43**, 401-406.

Report of the governor's committee on the defense of insanity. *New York Law Journal*, 1958, **140**, nos. 5 & 6.

Resnick, P. Child murder by parents. *American Journal of Psychiatry*, 1969, **126**, 325-334.

——. Murder of the newborn. *American Journal of Psychiatry*, 1970, **126**, 1414-1420.

Robin, G. D. Justifiable homicide by police officers. *Journal of Criminal Law, Criminology, and Police Science*, 1963, **54**, 225-231.

Robinson, G. W. A study of political assassination.

American Journal of Psychiatry, 1965, **121**, 1060-1064.

Rokeach, M. *The three Christs of Ypsilanti.* New York: Knopf, 1964.

Rosenbaum, J., & Richman, R. Suicide. *American Journal of Psychiatry,* 1970, **126**, 1652-1655.

Rothstein, D. A. Presidential assassination syndrome. *Archives of General Psychiatry,* 1964, **11**, 245-255.

Rudin, S. A. National motives predict psychogenic death rates 25 years later. *Science,* 1968, **160**, 901-903.

Ruotolo, A. Dynamics of sudden murder. *American Journal of Psychoanalysis,* 1968, **28**, 162-176.

Sargent, D. Children who kill. *Social Work,* 1962, **7**(1), 35-42.

Sayed, Z. A., Lewis, S. A., & Brittain, R. P. An electroencephalographic and psychiatric study of 32 insane murderers. *British Journal of Psychiatry,* 1969, **115**, 1115-1124.

Scherl, D. J. & Mack, J. E. A study of adolescent matricide. *Journal of the American Academy of Child Psychiatry,* 1966, **5**, 569-593.

Schilder, P. The attitudes of murderers toward death. *Journal of Abnormal and Social Psychology,* 1936, **31**, 348-363.

Schipkowensky, N. Affective disorders. *International Psychiatry Clinics,* 1968, **5**(3), 59-75.

Schrag, C. Critical analysis of sociological theories. In D. Mulvihill, M. Tumin, & L. Curtis (Eds.), *Crimes of violence, volume 13.* Washington, D.C.: United States Government Printing Office, 1969. Pp. 1241-1290.

Schuessler, K. F. The deterrent influence of the death

penalty. *Annals of the American Academy of Political Science,* 1952, **284,** 54-62.

Scott, J. P. Critical periods in behavioral development. *Science,* 1962, **138,** 949-958.

Smith, S. The adolescent murderer. *Archives of General Psychiatry,* 1965, **13,** 310-319.

Stafford-Clark, D., & Taylor, F. H. Clinical and electro-encephalographic studies of prisoners charged with murder. *Journal of Neurology, Neurosurgery and Psychiatry,* 1949, **12,** 325-330.

Stern, E. S. The Medea complex. *Journal of Mental Science,* 1948, **94,** 321-331.

Szasz, T. *Ideology and insanity.* Garden City, N.Y.: Doubleday, 1969.

Tanay, E. Psychiatric aspects of homicide prevention. *American Journal of Psychiatry,* 1972, **128,** 815-818.

Teele, J. E. Measure of social participation. *Social Problems,* 1962, **10,** 31-39.

———. Suicidal behavior, assaultiveness, and socialization principles. *Social Forces,* 1965, **43,** 510-518.

Ward, D. A., Jackson, M., & Ward, R. E. Crimes of violence by women. In D. Mulvihill, M. Tumin, & L. Curtis (Eds.), *Crimes of violence, volume 13.* Washington, D.C.: United States Government Printing Office, 1969. Pp. 843-910.

Weinstein, E. A., & Lyerly, O. Symbolic aspects of presidential assassination. *Psychiatry,* 1969, **32,** 1-11.

Weiss, J. M. A., Lamberti, J. W., & Blackman, N. The sudden murderer. *Archives of General Psychiatry,* 1960, **2,** 669-678.

Weisz, A. E., & Taylor, R. American presidential assassinations. *Diseases of the Nervous System,* 1969, 30, 659-668.

West, D. *Murder followed by suicide.* Cambridge: Harvard University Press, 1966.

Williams, D. Neural factors related to habitual aggression. *Brain,* 1969, 93, 503-520.

Wilmer, H. A. "Murder, you know." *Psychiatric Quarterly,* 1969, 43, 1-34.

Wittman, O., & Astrachan, M. Psychological investigation of a homicidal youth. *Journal of Clinical Psychology,* 1949, 5, 88-93.

Wolfgang, M. Husband-wife homicide. *Journal of Social Therapy,* 1956, 2, 263-271.

———. Victim-precipitated criminal homicide. *Journal of Criminal Law, Criminology, and Police Science,* 1957, 48, 1-11.

———. *Patterns of criminal homicide.* Philadelphia: University of Pennsylvania Press, 1958.

———. *Studies in homicide.* New York: Harper & Row, 1967.

———. Suicide by means of victim-precipitated homicide. In H. Resnick (Ed.), *Suicidal behaviors.* Boston: Little Brown, 1969.

Wolfgang, M., & Ferracuti, F. Subculture of violence. *International Annals of Criminology,* 1962, 1, 1-9.

Wood, A. L. A socio-structural analysis of murder, suicide, and economic crime in Ceylon. *American Sociological Review,* 1961, 26, 744-753.

Woods, S. M. Adolescent violence and homicide. *Archives of General Psychiatry,* 1961, 5, 528-534.

Wulfften-Palthe, P. M. Amok. *Nederlands Tijdschrift voor Geneeskunde,* 1933, 7, 983.

Author index

Subject index

About the authors

David Lester, Ph.D.

Dr. David Lester is associate professor of psychology at Stockton State College, Pomona, New Jersey. Previously he was director of research at the Suicide Prevention and Crisis Service in Buffalo.

Dr. Lester was educated at Cambridge University, where he earned B.A. and M.A. degrees, and at Brandeis University, where he received M.A. and Ph.D. degrees.

Dr. Lester is the author of *Why People Kill Themselves.*

Gene Lester, Ph.D.

Dr. Gene Lester teaches at Stockton State College where she is assistant professor of psychology. She has also taught at Wheaton College, Norton, Massachusetts, and State University College, Buffalo, New York.

Dr. Lester was educated at Occidental College and Brandeis University, where she earned her Ph.D.

Dr. David Lester and Dr. Gene Lester are co-authors of *Suicide: The Gamble with Death.*